trative

y us

respo   s   l on their ticke

or damag   st be paid for as required by the
rian.

ks may be made to local librari
'bra

SOLDIER IN THE SADDLE

SOLDIER IN THE SADDLE

"MONKEY" BLACKER

BURKE  LONDON

ACKNOWLEDGMENT

The author and publishers are grateful to Messrs. William Collins Sons & Co. Ltd., for permission to quote from *The Struggle for Europe* by Chester Wilmot.

BURKE PUBLISHING CO. LTD.,
14, JOHN STREET, LONDON, W.C.1

Printed in Great Britain by
East Midland Printing Co. Ltd.
Bury St. Edmunds, Suffolk

Contents

List of Plates

Prologue

IT is an unsettling experience to have had two or three years of adult life before the Second World War began. You belong to a generation which is neither one thing nor the other. For older people the nineteen-thirties represent a period in which they were young, sowed their wild oats and perhaps got married—a part of their life divided by the war years from their middle age. Younger people grew up with or after the war. But we had a few tantalising moments in that other world, and just as we were beginning to enjoy ourselves all the fun ended.

I can remember clearly what those few short years were like, but I look back on the period as one to which I did not really belong, rather more like a play than real life. And a pretty far-fetched play too, not at all true to life as we know it now.

Books about the thirties sometimes give the impression that it was an age of protest, that people spent their time arguing passionately about Communism and Fascism, about rearmament, and foreign policy. British youth, it is now assumed, was seething with political ideas, and either rushing off to fight in Spain, or voting not to fight for anybody at all. A restless time, you might think, in which to live, and you would be wrong.

Most people jogged through life steadily and calmly, ignoring the warning cries of Winston Churchill, and regarding the antics of Oswald Mosley and his Fascists as merely a diversion to be enjoyed in the Sunday newspapers.

The Spanish Civil War rumbled away vaguely in the background. Then came Munich, and with it a shock to this atmosphere of unrealistic calm, but until the crisis broke the majority of British people had entirely failed to register that something unpleasant was about to happen. Their complacency was staggering.

The Army, still horsed, lived mainly in a world of its own. The threat of mechanisation, bitterly and unrealistically fought by the regiments affected, was the only discordant note in a cycle of sport and traditional routine. I joined the 5th Royal Inniskilling Dragoon Guards in 1936, and from then onwards my life moved contentedly along grooves worn smooth by cavalry custom. Each winter we all departed for two months to hunt; in the spring we rode in point-to-points to the accompaniment of not very exacting military duties, and during the summer we were mainly concerned with polo. In the autumn there were some fairly intensive manœuvres, after which the cycle began again.

Dilatory and inefficient, you might think, and again you would be wrong. In some strange way this routine produced year by year a regiment which—given modern equipment and more men—was obviously fit to fight. This surprising result was achieved by senior officers who, operating admittedly in a far less complicated world, had a much better grasp of essentials than their modern counterparts. The discipline they imposed was impersonal, strict and fair; they had enough self-confidence to go their own way without too much regard for the opinions of their superiors. They dealt with the essentials and very sensibly spent the rest of their time enjoying themselves. From their example I learnt a lesson early in life which I have since tried to follow.

After three years of this comparatively idyllic existence, war swept away all the old landmarks. The wartime years accelerated and vitalised the tempo of life. The barriers between the Army and the world outside were broken down; I had to think of something other than horses to talk about. I realised that until 1940 I had been intellectually only half awake.

By the time of my marriage immediately after the war, this new outlook had fused with memories of the dream world before the deluge, and had become dominated by a sense of wasted time. I began to combine my life as a soldier with the activities of which I had dreamed and been deprived during the war. This book describes, from 1937 to the present day, some of the highlights of the past twenty-five years.

Most of my story, though not all, centres round the horse. There was a time when I, as a small boy, was not particularly keen on riding, and would without encouragement have probably given it up. My mother and father provided exactly the right stimulus and example, and I persevered. I thus received the priceless advantage of having ridden, and ridden hard, since I was five years old. Since then I have so often blessed my parents for a gift which I did not appreciate fully at the time, but which has since brought me much that is good.

CHAPTER ONE

Rareweed

THIS is the story of the first horse I ever owned. His personality, and the ups and downs which we experienced together, provide some of my clearest memories of the pre-war years.

Rareweed and I first went into partnership when I was nineteen and he was seven. He had come to my father's stable from a well-known training establishment, which he had left under a cloud. His relations with the authorities there, we understood, had for some time been deteriorating. They were eventually severed after Rareweed had decided to "go slow", a policy which, though it did credit to his strength of character, detracted from his value as a race-horse.

My father, who was well known for his skill in rejuvenating bored racehorses, eventually took Rareweed as a gift. Then, in the spirit of "Let's see what the boy can do with him", and presumably feeling it was time I had a horse of my own, my father passed him on to me.

Rareweed was born in France, of distinguished parents. In his youth he had often featured at the smarter French race-meetings, and upon one summer day at Longchamps he had achieved what was ever to remain the highlight of his career by running fifth in the French Derby. Gradually, however, it became apparent that he was not likely to prove an outstanding success in the flat-racing world, and he was sold to England to see if hurdling would suit him better. It did not. His physical powers had probably been impaired by being raced too often and too young in France, but in any case he soon made it clear that he disliked intensely the rough, cold, winter sport which seemed to earn him nothing but rapped shins and smacked quarters. He failed conspicuously to make his mark in this new sphere.

When he first came to me he was all too clearly a throwout: a piece of the equine flotsam which the racing world tosses on one side in such profusion during its onward march. His once-elegant figure was hollow and angular, and in his aristocratic eye all the original softness had been replaced by a wary suspicion. He, who had once been valuable and sought after, was now valueless; once willing to do his best, he was now sullenly determined not to co-operate.

I, however, was delighted with him. Here was a racehorse of distinguished breeding, temporarily under a cloud perhaps, but still an acquisition of which to be proud. And when, shortly after his arrival, I went to Colchester to join my regiment for the first time, Rareweed came too. There, in surroundings equally strange to both of us, we got to know each other.

Until then I had not realised to what lengths equine non-co-operation, when practised by a master, could be carried. Rareweed was not in the least vicious, in fact he was on the whole amiably disposed towards me, but he was on principle opposed to any kind of forward movement. Experience had taught him that it was inadvisable to gallop, since he might then be expected to race against other horses, with all the undesirable implications on which he was now an expert. His policy, therefore, was so to exhaust his rider while progressing through the slower paces that a gallop could never be achieved. This he practised by sheer inertia, aided by a hide which the strong arms of jockeys on both sides of the Channel had apparently converted into a sort of armour-plating.

Thus for some weeks the only way in which I could induce my classically-bred racehorse to accelerate from a walk to a trot was by employing tactics more appropriate to a Donkey Derby. As his strength and spirits returned, and when he saw I did not as yet wish him to gallop, his attitude improved, but it never became enthusiastic.

Soon I began taking him out with the local hounds. He initially regarded hunting, as he did almost every activity, with an air of deep suspicion. He would only consent to jump very small obstacles, and then only after he had personally assured himself that there was no hazard, however slight, on the far side which could cause him any discomfort or inconvenience. This was an improvement on his performance at home, where he regarded jumping as something at which he totally drew the line; indeed a small pole a foot from the ground would produce in him a reluctance so decisive that one might have thought he was being invited to jump off the cliffs of Dover. Out hunting he occasionally showed a mild enthusiasm, but in general his attitude was tolerant and indulgent, like a good-natured grown-up at a party who consents to join in the children's games so long as they do not become rough and rude.

After I had had him nearly a year he began to look really well again, and I thought it was time to see how he would view running in a point-to-point. I was not particularly optimistic by this time, and thought that he was all too likely to refuse to negotiate the first fence, but I was determined to try. I accordingly entered him in a novice's race at an Aldershot Military Meeting at Tweseldown. In those days, when most of the Army was still horsed, all races there were confined to soldiers, and this particular race was about as modest a contest as could be found.

On the appointed day it poured with rain and the course became a morass. Wearing a pained and surprised expression, Rareweed cantered delicately through the mud jumped reasonably willingly and finished third. Quite obviously he had not exerted himself in the slightest.

Encouraged by this comparative success, I then took him to another point-to-point, in which he was second. I then threw caution to the winds and entered him in the Aldershot Open Cup, the blue riband of the military point-to-point world. Here we would meet horses several classes better than anything that we had encountered up to date, and it was made clear to me that one or two of my brother-officers regarded my action as slightly presumptuous for one in his first season.

"At any rate," I thought to myself as I stood, rather over-awed, in the paddock before mounting, "he's the best-looking horse in the race." This indeed was true; he had regained much of his Longchamps bloom and looked a real aristocrat. But when the race started he did not behave like one. "This racing business is becoming too much of a habit," he had apparently decided, and wearing a discontented expression he cantered along well in the rear of the field, totally ignoring my urgings.

The last three furlongs of the Tweseldown course are uphill, and by the time the rest of the field had reached this point we were almost a fence behind them. I felt overwhelmed with mortification. This was a most ignominious end to the venture; how foolish I had been to build my hopes so high, and how right my brother-officers were being proved. A spasm of fury took hold of me; suddenly I saw red, turned in my saddle and, with an arm to which rage had given unnatural strength, dealt Rareweed's quarters two fearful smacks. With a gasp of surprise he bounded forward, shaken from his normal composure. Equally surprised and still enraged, I drove him forward with every ounce of energy I had. Suddenly he began to travel like a horse possessed—I had not thought that anything could gallop uphill so fast. Here was the real speed that had been lying latent, acceleration like a Bentley bearing down upon a gaggle of Minicars. But the leading Minicars were desperately near the finish even if travelling at half the speed;

those in the rear flicked back past me like telegraph poles being left behind by a train, but still there were two which surely could never be caught.

My frantic, flying figure turned into the straight as they were jumping the last fence, swooped upon and overtook the rearmost of the two. A few crowded seconds later Rareweed's nose passed the post exactly level with that of his rival, and a dead heat was proclaimed. It was in every sense a breathtaking finish; the crowd and our opponents were almost speechless with surprise at our unexpected appearance, I was quite speechless with exhaustion and even Rareweed was slightly out of breath.

It was a great moment for me, for not only was it my first victory (if such a dead heat can be called) but I had tied with the combination, celebrated in the military racing world, of Major Roscoe Harvey as rider and Lieutenant-Colonel Willoughby Norrie as owner, both of the 10th Hussars. They were very kind to me, particularly the owner, who insisted despite my protests that I should have sole possession of an enormous silver cup. When I sit, as I do now, at meetings of the National Hunt Committee and look across at my fellow member, the distinguished Lord Norrie, I often remember that race at Aldershot and the kindly act which put the seal on a very happy day for a young subaltern many years ago. Once I asked him if he remembered too; sad to say, he has no recollection of the occasion at all!

I returned to Aldershot in a high state of elation, and doubtless rather too big for my boots. There is, however, a Fate whose special duty it is to deal with young men who think their star is in the ascendant. My next engagement with Rareweed was the Regimental Race, and after my success at Aldershot practically every man in the regiment backed me. For the first time I realised how very different it is to ride a horse on which you apparently cannot lose, from riding one on which everyone will be amazed if you win.

On this occasion the third obstacle was a fence with a ditch in front of it, and for some reason this ditch had no guard-rail before it to show the horses where to take off. This, in a point-to-point, was a fair hazard, but it struck Rareweed as being altogether outside trade union rules. Thus the onlookers were almost at once regaled with the spectacle of their fancy peering fearfully into the depths of the ditch while the race disappeared into the distance. They were not pleased, and made this fact clear to me as I returned ignominiously to the paddock. On this slightly unsatisfactory note the season ended.

I then thought that since he was so quiet to ride he might fill in his time next autumn by acting as a charger on parade. Accordingly the day came when he was clothed in glittering saddlery, equipped with a sword, hung with a flowing plume and ridden forth on a "regimental drill". But this unpredictable animal, totally unmoved by the flurry and excitement of the hunting field, and bored almost to tears by the hectic atmosphere of a race-meeting, was entranced by the martial scene which now confronted him.

With gleaming eye he cavorted to and fro, bucking in a most disconcerting fashion and trying in his quieter moments to eat his plume. Whilst accompanying my troop to the parade-ground he developed an overmastering passion for a female troop-horse in the front row. He made determined efforts to introduce himself to her, much to the prejudice of good order and military discipline, and by the time we reached our destination there were already signs of confusion in the ranks.

Once on parade, my charger strongly objected to standing out in solitary state in front of the troop. Quivering with excitement, he backed convulsively into the front rank, in search of his girl-friend. When his quarters touched another horse, he kicked it. Soon he had put the whole troop to flight, and the senior officers in charge of the parade became conscious of a wave of disorder spreading through a large part of the parade-ground.

I was soon at the receiving end of one of those tornadic rebukes in which pre-war senior Cavalry officers specialised, and which left both giver and receiver white and shaken, the one from passion, the other from fright. I sadly mounted a troop-horse, and my erstwhile charger, still with a rollicking look in his eye, was led hastily away.

My plans for the next racing season were comprehensive and drawn up with the greatest care. I had, in my dead heat at Aldershot, surmounted the only peak that was then within my horizon, and now another and higher mountain had come into view. My new objective was Sandown Park itself, and to this eminence I proposed to advance methodically and by stages.

Rareweed's preparation went forward smoothly, the weather smiled, the entries were sent in, the season was nearly upon us. Not a ripple marred the perfection of my arrangements. There was no hitch of any kind. My programme was mapped out to the smallest detail; all that remained was to implement it. Complacently, I waited for my first engagement.

Of course, if I had known as much about racing then as I do now I should not have been complacent at all. I should have been deeply suspicious. Nothing, in my experience, is so potentially disastrous as a situation which promises to develop exactly as planned, and upon which high hopes and ambitions have been based. Expect everything and you will get nothing. Begin well and you will end badly. Hope for little and you may get a little—at least you will not be too disappointed if you do not. And sometimes, just very occasionally, if you do not despair and if you keep on trying, you may get a lot. That, of course, is why people like racing.

I now need hardly say that my high hopes on this occasion were not fulfilled. My plans were frustrated and laid in ruins. I rode not one winner of any kind during the season and, indeed, was never even placed. It was to be ten years (not all, admittedly, spent in racing) before I entered the winner's enclosure at Sandown. However, this was all probably very good for me.

The immediate cause of Rareweed's failure that season was the weather, which was delightful. But unfortunately it made the ground hard. In my first race of the season I became miserably conscious that the Rareweed who had skimmed magnificently through the mud was temporarily no more. His easy sweep had been replaced by an unhappy, jerky scratch; his unwillingness had become redoubled. As the expression goes, he liked it soft.

His second race of the season was the regimental Subalterns' Race, and the modest ability of his opponents made me feel that here at least, despite the ground which was by now rock-hard, we could win. The course, a clearly marked circle, was an easy one, and after we had gone some distance I was just behind the leading horse and beginning to challenge it.

The two of us swung into the straight with about three fences to go. My rival, now a distinguished General, began to ride his hardest. So did I. The finish rapidly became epic —whips flying, teeth set, both of us deaf to the shouts of the crowd which was doubtless by now beside itself with excitement. We passed the post locked together. "Another dead heat," I thought disgustedly. Then, struck by a curious lack of enthusiasm in the crowd, I looked back. With a feeling of nausea I beheld the rest of the field virtuously galloping round the second circuit of the course. My groom walked up to take my horse, his face expressionless. The comparative silence of the onlookers was broken. "Thank God," said a loud voice with feeling, "we've got a Navy."

I soon found that the race had been not only a fiasco, but a disaster. Rareweed was lame. The contest between his legs and the hard ground had ended in a decisive victory for the latter, and there could be no question of running him again that year. His tendons were fired and he withdrew from the public gaze until the opening of the next hunting season, by which time he was fully recovered.

On a November day Rareweed and I were out hunting. He was beginning to take a mild interest in the chase by this time, and would even jump fences without first reconnoitring them for possible hazards. On this occasion we had been held up in a queue for a gateway, and in order to get a good start I decided to pull out and jump a fence nearby. It seemed quite a straightforward obstacle and Rareweed consented to jump it without hesitation. We took off—into a nightmare. Glinting below us on the landing side was a long strand of new barbed wire, firmly attached to posts and stretching the whole length of the fence. Rareweed landed, and before he could take another stride the wire was biting into his forelegs. He did not fall, but staggered frantically forward. For one sickening moment I saw the whole fence being carried forward into the field by our momentum, and heard the protesting screech of the wire as it took the strain. At last we stopped. I got off.

As I was later to learn in the war, a sudden catastrophe seems to produce in one a feeling of detachment, presumably designed to carry one through the first trying moments. Without any sense of shock I observed that Rareweed's upper forelegs were cut to the bone and savagely lacerated. Almost casually, I removed the wire and contemplated the ruin to which I had reduced my friend. He was just able to hobble very slowly, and to a nearby motor horsebox we painfully made our way. He had to be almost lifted into it, and when we got home he was so stiff that it took us a long time to get him out again. The vet arrived and without hesitation pronounced sentence of death. Very soon afterwards it was carried out.

That November day is separated from the present by a gulf of almost a quarter of a century, including six years passed amid the tragedy of a World War. Nevertheless, I can still recapture the sense of grief, self-reproach and shock which I experienced for some time after this disaster. At that time it was easily the worst thing that had happened to me.

An odd sense of proportion, perhaps, to get so upset about a horse. But he had trusted me and I had let him down. I had spent much of our time together trying to persuade him that jumping a fence involved nothing very dreadful, only to end up by killing him in barbed wire. I consoled myself by thinking that at least I had, in Rareweed's time with me, provided some of the few rays of sunshine in his bleak existence.

I was lucky as a young man to own a horse of my own, and perhaps luckier still that I was not provided with a beautifully-schooled mount on which I could score with little effort over my fellows. Fortunate indeed is the young man who has to learn the hard way.

And if his partner provides him, as mine did, with a stock of affectionate memories which can be brought out from time to time, examined and returned to store with a smile, the young man is luckier still. Rareweed may not have won me much money, but he left me a fairly substantial legacy all the same.

CHAPTER TWO

Expeditionary Force, 1940

ONE day in the spring of 1939 my Colonel refused me permission to ride in a point-to-point. I was horrified—this was unthinkable, particularly since I was almost certain to win. But no, my Colonel was adamant. There were more important duties for me to perform, he said, and a very shaken subaltern withdrew to ponder the sudden realisation that, despite the Munich anti-climax, life was becoming serious.

The loss of our horses on mechanisation had been regarded as inevitable, and did not convey the same sense of desolation to the younger members of the regiment as it had to the older ones. Many of the latter were in fact unmechanisable and promptly left—the rest of us greeted the arrival of our new 5-ton tanks and carriers with resignation. Life was at first not greatly changed. Presumably with the intention of keeping us in a good humour—there can surely have been no other reason—each officer retained a charger. The regiment's role was to form the Divisional Cavalry of an infantry division, to provide the reconnaissance, and the advance and rearguards, as we had done for so long on horses.

However, as the international situation darkened, the atmosphere changed. Colonel "Ugly" Martin, affable, explosive, and with the kindest of hearts, had perceived clearly the urgency of our situation. We had, he estimated, a year in which to master the techniques of mechanisation. He was perfectly right, and a great many of us would not be alive today without the knowledge and expertise which was so drastically drummed into us during the summer of 1939. But at the time it was a shock to find our normal life so rudely disrupted.

We were at camp near Shorncliffe when, in August, the news of the Hitler-Stalin pact came through, and from that moment it was assumed that in a matter of days we would be at war. Colonel Martin was promoted out of our sight and Colonel Jack Anstice, very much the martinet, reigned in his stead. Mobilisation followed and the next few days passed in receiving and sorting out the flood of reservists who soon began to pour through the barrack gates. Most of them were so excited about this sudden upheaval in their lives and the renewal of old friendships that they were at this stage not at all downcast—indeed they were in an extremely hilarious mood. They retained from civilian life a very independent frame of mind, and it took days of arduous and tactful toil before they could even be got into the right barrack block, still less coaxed on to the parade-ground and sorted out.

Thus we were very fully occupied, and the departure of our chargers—short-lived perquisites—seemed just another event and not the disaster it would earlier have appeared. The days rushed forward hectically until the invasion of Poland, then forty-eight hours of growing suspense during which another Munich seemed, appallingly, not to be out of the question—and there we were grouped round the mess wireless set listening to the reedy tones of Mr Chamberlain announcing war.

My first impression of wartime life was that it was easily the most expensive venture that I had ever embarked upon. Every tradesman in London and Colchester realised at once what an exceptionally bad financial bet were young officers on the outbreak of war, and demanded settlement with un-precedented firmness. Living as we did on a precarious scaffolding of credit and hire purchase which now dis-integrated sharply beneath us, we were sorely harassed. Not all our problems could be solved as easily as my hire-purchase car, which was immediately returned whence it came; the total effect of all these bills arriving simul-taneously, accompanied by threats which were often not even veiled, was crushing. Men in bowler hats, their pockets bulging with writs, became a common sight in the barracks. Officers developed hunted and furtive looks; the news of our almost immediate departure to France was loudly cheered from motives not entirely patriotic. This departure, and some generous parental help, saved my bacon and, my ears still ringing with the noise of financial chickens coming home to roost, I said goodbye to my happy pre-war world.

The British Expeditionary Force assembled uneventfully in northern Europe in the autumn of 1939. Until the ex-plosion in May, 1940, we became engaged in what has variously been called the *Sitzkrieg*, the Phoney War, or the Twilight War. This, from the BEF's point of view, was a good thing, for it at least gave us time to train into some semblance of an army the collection of regulars, reservists and national service men who had been mixed together and decanted on to the muddy plains of northern France.

Point and urgency were given to our training by reports of Panzer divisions concentrating in the Aachen area, by the reconnaissance flights which German aircraft regularly made, and by alarmist rumours flowing over the nearby frontier from neutral Belgium. From the villages in which we were billeted our light tanks and carriers would daily rattle forth to exercise, and soon the names of La Bassée, Armentières, Givenchy and Aubers rang as naturally in our ears as in those of our predecessors twenty years before. Indeed the whole countryside was peopled with ghosts from Flanders fields; we soaked up the atmosphere in a way that was almost macabre, but oddly affecting and inspiring.

Winter closed in on us in our farmhouses and villas: the

winter of U-boat warfare and jokes about the black-out; of
Finland, and *We'll hang out the washing on the Siegfried
Line*; the winter of amateur war. Christmas, though celebrated far from home, was a happy one; we were trained
and ready, news of English leave was cheering. At that
moment our morale was at its highest; in the New Year
disillusion, doubt and boredom begun to set in and the
spirit of the BEF sank slowly till it was rekindled by Hitler
in May, 1940.

During the winter, which soon became one of the coldest
in memory, we experienced three false alarms of invasion,
occurrences which became known as "flaps". The first took
place in thick fog, the second in deep snow, and the third,
at last, in reasonable weather. On the first two occasions
no one, at any rate at regimental level, seriously thought
anything was going to happen, but each time we rushed
frenziedly to the frontier in accordance with pre-arranged
plans. There we would wait, the sense of anti-climax strong
upon us, until we were told to find billets nearby and await
developments. Slowly the excitement and interest would
subside and leave us usually worse housed than formerly.
(I need hardly say that when the real invasion came we got
no warning at all, merely hearing the announcement on
the BBC.)

By March we had had our fill of training and of false
alarms. The suspicion grew that we were forgotten men,
that there would indeed, as many military commentators
were saying, be "no war in the West". The spotlight was
fixed on Finland, the Balkans, the Middle East, anywhere
but on us. A feeling of frustrated boredom began to
flourish; nothing, even the fleshpots of Lille, was fun any
more; some of us talked of volunteering to fight the
Russians in Finland.

May came and our plans for the summer even included
polo. My turn arrived for a fortnight's leave in England,
and with my friend Humphrey Philips I crossed from
Boulogne, leaving a bored and disillusioned regiment

behind us. It did not seem possible or likely that anything would happen now.

I was in the most comfortable place in the world, my bed at home. It was eight o'clock in the morning, and outside the window was a row of elm trees bathed in sunshine. It was nice lying in bed looking at those elms, and I wondered idly how many times I had lain like this, on a bright, sunny holiday morning, looking at those old trees. Coming on leave from France was much like coming back from school, really. Except that France was even duller than school. A pity we were all getting stale, bored with flaps that never came to anything, bored with training, and bored with each other. Anyway, no need to worry for twelve lovely days. For this was my first leave morning, a beautiful sunny May morning, the morning of 10th May, 1940.

The telephone was ringing downstairs. Someone answered it, and then my mother popped her head round the door. "It's for you," she said. At eight o'clock in the morning? How very odd. I stumbled downstairs and soon I was listening to the urgent tones of Humphrey Philips. "Have you heard?" he asked. I mumbled a negative. "The balloon's gone up," he said crisply. "The Germans marched into the Low Countries this morning—it's on the news." Dazed with sleep and surprise, I continued to let Humphrey make the running. "We must go back—at once," he said.

There could be no question of disagreeing with him. The Big Moment, so long awaited and so often despaired of, was here. The Phoney War was ended. At this moment, whilst I stood dumbly grasping the receiver, the BEF would be moving across the Belgian frontier towards its appointed position on the River Dyle. In two or three days the regiment would be fighting its first battle of the Second World War. Armageddon, the Battle of the West, the Battle of France, the supreme experience, whatever you like to call it, of our lives, was at hand. And we were sitting at home, missing it. Intolerable that we should miss it. Yes, certainly we must go back—at once.

My father drove me to London to meet Humphrey, so that together we could accomplish the formality (as we imagined) of cutting our leave short and returning to duty. The War Office was in a turmoil, but eventually we penetrated into the office of the Staff Officer who dealt with leave problems. When we made our humble request, he gazed at us as if we had gone mad. "But you have twelve days to go," he kept repeating helplessly, "there is no *need* for you to go back. In any case it is quite impossible to bypass the normal channels in this way." I said that I was the Adjutant and that my stand-in was very inexperienced and would be sure to make a nonsense of it. The first part was true, but the second, Heaven help me, was most certainly not, as anyone who knows Frank Stockdale will realise. In any case, it cut no ice. The man was adamant. So was everyone else we tried. Soon it was lunchtime.

With desperate faces we plodded dismally down Piccadilly towards the Cavalry Club. LILLE BOMBED shrieked the headlines. Poor Lille, obviously a heap of ruins. No more lovely meals at the *Huitrière*; poor, glamorous Betty Spell crushed beneath the ruins of her night club. (I need hardly say our fears were groundless.) BRITISH TROOPS MOVE INTO BELGIUM, THE GERMANS ADVANCE—with each step we took the headlines mocked at and increased our impotent fury. On the steps of the Club we found friends, older men who had fought in the former war and who laughed at our impatience. "Good Heavens," they said, "go home and enjoy your leave. You will get plenty of fighting before this lot's over." Experienced advice, which we did not take. And for once experience was wrong, for if we had tamely gone home and returned twelve days later we would merely have become members of one of the many forlorn and helpless leave parties which, armed with rifles and five rounds a man, plodded round drearily and with no hope of ever finding their regiments, amid the chaos which France had by that time become.

Our assault upon the War Office was renewed after lunch, and until the late afternoon was repelled at all points. But at last we met our man, a man with a twinkle, a nice fat man, helpful and kind and all a Staff Officer should be—a paragon of a Staff Officer. He indicated that if we went to Dover the following morning with a piece of paper which he gave us, we *might* be able to slip unobtrusively aboard a ship there, a ship carrying very important Generals back to France, and probably the last ship to leave Dover for some time. This called for a celebration, which we duly had.

The Staff Officers aboard the ship were so intent on making certain that their particular Generals fetched up that they did not notice two cavalry subalterns with hangovers sneaking aboard. Soon we were docking at Boulogne, where a covey of staff cars met the Generals and whisked them away. Neither of us had the nerve to ask for a lift, and the problem of how to get to our next destination presented itself squarely before us.

I was, in fact, not at all clear what our next destination was. Being Adjutant, I should, I suppose, have known where the regiment was going to in Belgium, but beyond knowing that it would by now have been transferred from Fourth Division to Third and that it would be somewhere beyond Brussels, I had no idea at all of its probable whereabouts. On the whole it seemed best to go to Lille, where the rear party of Fourth Division would be, and seek information there.

But how? The trains did not seem to be functioning in the Lille direction, and the quayside was totally innocent of military transport. In fact the only vehicle in sight was an unpromising-looking taxi, and to this we made our way. Its dour driver regarded us impassively. Without much optimism we invited him to drive us the eighty miles to Lille. To our surprise and delight, no flicker of emotion crossed his face and all he said was *"Oui"*. But behind those porcine features his brain had been doing sums, and the final result of his calculations caused us to look thoughtfully at our stock of francs. But he had us cold—there was now no turning back, and it was not long before we were rattling uncomfortably down the *pavé* of the deserted Pas de Calais roads.

Somewhat to our disappointment Lille appeared, apart from a marked absence of the usual crowds of British military, to be perfectly normal. Fourth Division's rear party was still in its old headquarters, and in search of information I entered the presence of a Staff Officer who had instructed me at Sandhurst. He glanced up eagerly as I came in but looked unflatteringly disappointed when he saw who it was. "Did General X come with you?" he asked hopefully. I denied all knowledge of the General, and told him briefly of our recent movements. My recital seemed to enrage him; he launched into a tirade about whippersnappers occupying places on priority boats and stopping important Generals from taking part in vital campaigns—and pushed me out into the passage. A hardly less unfriendly officer then told us that since our regiment was now in Third Division he had no idea at all where it was. No, he had no transport at all. Back we went to our taxidriver, sitting impassively in the courtyard. Would he drive us another seventy miles to Brussels? This time the *"oui"* did not come out so readily; the sums took longer and the answer when it came was even more formidable. But our blood was up and we rattled off again, this time on Belgian *pavé*.

It was dark when we reached the centre of Brussels, which looked enticingly full of life. But in the distance searchlights forked up into the night sky, there was a curious thudding noise accompanied by flashes, and it became clear that there was an air-raid on. With a screech of brakes our taxi drew to a halt. The driver, a man of decision, had reached the conclusion that he had come far enough. In a matter of seconds we found ourselves standing on the pavement in the centre of the metropolis, with our late driver's tail-light fading rapidly into the gloom.

We boarded a Belgian taxi, and drove eastwards out of Brussels in search of the British. Three miles out we found a British military policeman who told us where the head-quarters of Third Division probably was. He did even better, he lent us a truck. We pressed on towards Louvain, plunged into a network of minor roads, got lost, and even-tually found, at two o'clock in the morning, the *château* in which Third Division Headquarters was reputed to be. It was not there. Nobody was there.

The determination and *élan* with which I had begun the day had by now evaporated, and I cravenly suggested bedding down in the truck until it got light. But Hum-phrey, inexhaustible and cheerful as always, would have none of this. Round and round the lanes we trundled, and at last, at long last, we found the headquarters. A sleepy Duty Officer was fetched. "Where is our regiment?" we demanded. "Erps-Querps," mumbled the officer. At three in the morning this sort of remark seemed uncalled for, and we brusquely told him not to be funny. "But that's where it is," he persisted in hurt tones. And a glance at the map showed us that it really was, only five miles away at that.

Dawn was breaking on Erps-Querps, covering with a misty dew the tanks and carriers clustered round the farm buildings. The guard, familiar faces in unfamiliar sur-roundings, grinned a welcome as they saw us. In the distance was the exciting mutter and crump of bombs. With a triumphant bang I set down my grip amid the slumbering officers in a nearby barn. Up rose a sleepy but outraged face, surmounted by beetling brows. "If you *must* come in at this God-forsaken hour," said a senior officer fiercely, "for God's sake don't make such a bloody row!" I was back.

And, what was more, back in plenty of time. After a

reasonably uneventful march into Belgium the regiment had reached the BEF's appointed forward position on the River Dyle. In front of them on the Albert Canal the Belgian Army was still holding the Germans; British and German troops were not destined to clash for another twenty-four hours after our return. I resumed my duties as Adjutant almost as if nothing had happened.

Very soon it became apparent that the morale and resistance of the Belgians were crumbling rapidly. The first manifestation had been the arrival of refugees, first in a trickle and soon swelling into a flood. During the day after my return all the roads leading westwards became choked with a slowly moving and rapidly thickening mass of traffic. High farm wagons drawn by teams of great Flemish horses, their harness gay with brass and ribbons, creaked along laden with a pathetic burden of personal possessions and children still clinging to the toys with which they had been playing when panic struck their homes. Motors crammed with suitcases and strange, shapeless bundles, and almost invariably topped by a canopy of striped mattresses tied on with scraps of rope, chugged slowly along with frequent checks and halts. Scores of cyclists, their machines hung from handlebars to mudguards with packages, wound their way through the column. Aged peasants trudged on foot, silent and expressionless. None seemed to know where they were going; they were impelled by a quiet pervasive terror inspired presumably by memories of 1914.

More sinister still, in the shifting pattern of the column a thin thread of Belgian soldiers became visible, also moving westwards. Overhead, round Louvain and neighbouring villages, droned German bombers. We strained to put the last touches to our defences on the River Dyle, realising that action was at last not far away. As we prepared ourselves, on every road there began to appear long columns of retreating Belgian soldiery—cavalry, horse-drawn artillery and infantry with horse-drawn transport—all crowding in upon the crossings over the river, treading upon the heels of the refugees, almost frantic with rumours of German parachute landings. As a fighting force they were, for the moment, finished; most were incoherent and with a wealth of dramatic and hopeless gestures they talked wildly of the battle on the Albert Canal, and of their horror of the German dive-bombers.

One afternoon I was keeping listening watch on our headquarters radio, and noticed that the passing flood of Belgian soldiery had dried up. The unnatural silence was broken by a crackling voice from my wireless announcing that our neighbouring regiment, the Fifteenth-Nineteenth Hussars, had made contact with advancing German infantry ten miles away. This provoked a very curious feeling in me; for the first time in my life there, within a few miles of me, were people whom, as soon as I saw them, I must try to kill, and who would likewise try to kill me. It was a thoughtful moment.

The Colonel and I drove forward to our positions along the river. The crews of the tanks and carriers had heard the news, and were in that curious tensed-up state, almost of exaltation, which sometimes seizes soldiers before battle, particularly their first battle. Boys had suddenly become men, and the spirit of loyalty, comradeship and team spirit shone forth from the lines of eager, generous faces in a way which I have never forgotten. As evening drew on, the first bursts of machine-gun and rifle fire broke the stillness and spread along the Dyle. By nightfall we were fully engaged in battle.

Round the ancient city of Louvain we had, for the next few days, our first taste of war. It was not a very severe engagement, our casualties were few and we held our ground without much difficulty. We soon grew accustomed to judging the direction and height of a shell from its whistle, and to estimating how far from us was a burst of fire; we noted them subconsciously and only reacted when necessary. We no longer jumped and ducked without cause. The Germans inspired in us no awe—they were tough and resourceful but unimaginative; provided we remembered our training we could deal with them. It soon became clear, however, that our fate depended on events further south.

Here a most perilous situation was developing—with great rapidity. On the right of the Armies in Belgium, the German armour had broken through, and was making alarming progress into France. Unless the Armies in Belgium were to be withdrawn with some speed there was every chance of the Germans outflanking them. An unattractive choice faced the High Command, who wisely decided that retreat was the only practicable alternative to disaster.

So the retreat began, from river-line to river-line, in a rhythm which seldom varied. The infantry would pull back at night, leaving us to cover them. At dawn we would withdraw ourselves, delaying and harassing the enemy until the bridges over the next obstacle were crossed and blown behind us. The infantry would resist the enemy on the river-line until, as invariably happened, events on our flanks forced the whole process to begin again for fear of encirclement. On several occasions we were nearly encircled ourselves, and cut off from our bridges. Co-ordination with our allies on the flanks was far from good, and often a patrol, sent to make contact with them, would find not only that they had gone but that German motor-cycles and armoured cars were thrusting enthusiastically round behind us through an open flank.

It was a wearying, frustrating business, to be always forced to retreat because of events over which we had no control. Hard as the Germans pressed us, we gave as good as we got; our training and discipline stood the test; our communications, despite our primitive wireless sets, never seriously failed. The resilience and quick reactions of our Colonel and his senior commanders extricated us time and again from crisis—they were indeed the embodiment of the old order of cavalry—officers "made supple in mind and body by the exertions and hazards of the hunting-field, polo-ground and race-course"; men schooled to use initiative and to think and act for themselves. The quality of our commanders was the greatest of many factors contributing to our remarkably low casualty figure during three continuous weeks of heavy fighting. For this quality their pre-war cavalry training, nowadays derided in some quarters, was responsible.

During our withdrawal across Belgium we retained our confidence that all would eventually be well. The revered French Army would recover and launch a counterstroke; our retreat was a case of *reculer pour mieux sauter*. This was the first and more orderly part of the retreat to Dunkirk, divided from the second, increasingly chaotic, part by a hiatus of two or three days of comparative inaction, days in which the scales fell from our eyes.

Our recrossing of the French frontier provided scenes which were a direct pointer to the calamity to come. At the frontier post, ironically named Risquet Tout, the familiar stream of refugees from Belgium met another, equally panic-stricken stream trying to enter Belgium from France. Dreadful news from the south had launched a flood of distracted French refugees northwards; now the two streams had met head on and almost congealed. Limousines containing sleek but agitated businessmen, carts, peasants on foot, trucks piled high with humanity and livestock merged, almost motionless, into one sweating, heaving, frightened, shouting mass. Only by taking to the fields could we get past this disturbing symptom of what lay before us, and as we drove back into France the sense of foreboding deepened. The factory towns of Tourcoing and Roubaix were almost deserted. The desolation of abandoned houses, the empty tramlines, the shuttered shops, the awful degrading scenes we had just witnessed, were a sickening indication of French morale.

Our destination had been our favourite billet of the Phoney War, a prosperous suburb of Lille. Now its villas lay open and deserted. Unmade beds and tables bearing

B

half-eaten meals testified to the haste with which their owners had taken flight. Everywhere was silence; not a welcome from any familiar door. At the first alarm our smooth and well-to-do friends had crammed themselves into their expensive cars and headed for the Riviera, leaving nothing but a trail of weeping domestics, disordered furniture and raided cellars. We settled back uneasily into this altered scene, our deepening apprehension relieved by the novelty of being in Corps reserve and having, for once, little to do but wait for instructions.

In fact, the next few days were anxious and unhappy. We had been under heavy pressure and were reacting; most had an overmastering desire to sleep. To perform the simplest duty required an effort of will. Across the frontier in Belgium the retreat had temporarily ceased, and the five regular British infantry divisions, gallant and battered, faced and held in close combat the triumphant German onrush. Elsewhere the news grew steadily worse.

One morning we learnt that the 9th French Army, immediately to our south, had disintegrated. Arras, lately the Headquarters of the BEF, had fallen, so had Amiens. Through a breach of sixty miles the German armour was driving towards our rear, and the sea. The Armies in Flanders had been almost separated from the main French forces in central France. To our north the Belgians were being borne back by ceaseless pressure; Holland had capitulated some days before. We still did not really believe the writing on the wall. This just could not happen. The great French Army *must* rally, as in 1914 it would stage a Marne, the front would somehow be stabilised.

The possibility of evacuation never crossed our minds at this stage. Colonel Anstice assembled his regiment and spoke to them that afternoon, informally gathered in the shade of a tree. He congratulated and thanked us all for what we had done in Belgium, and he described as fully as he was able the dangers ahead. It was clear that he was preparing us for what seemed at the time most likely to befall us, encirclement and a fight to the end. He closed with the words: "And if we have to go down, as we may, I know I can count on you to go down as the naval chaps do, with guns firing and flag flying." Trite words perhaps, unremarkable oratory, but they were so evidently inspired by loyalty, love and iron determination—and the sense of occasion was so tremendous—that his address remains with me as the one that has moved me most in all my Army service.

Now the comparatively orderly and regular withdrawals gave place, as far as we were concerned, to a hectic to and fro to stop up gaps and to support those hardest pressed. The five regular divisions had now been reinforced with some territorial divisions, brave but hopelessly untrained and underarmed. These took over the flanks of our diminishing salient and soon found themselves in grave trouble from German tanks. We were very far from being able to act the part of a rescuing force, for the bullets from our light tanks bounced harmlessly off the side of our German opponents. But through subterfuge, speed and calculated boldness we harried and delayed them, allowing the exhausted infantry to slip back behind us, seldom resting and never remaining long under one division.

I personally reached the stage when resignation became my armour and a dull determination my motive power. I subconsciously assumed that most of my friends and probably myself would shortly be killed. Every day which found us still alive was a bonus, casualties no more than a dull ache in emotions which had lost all their sensitivity in the battering and tension of the past fortnight. As Adjutant I stood beside the Colonel, best able of anyone to appreciate the strain which this sensitive and highly-strung martinet kept miraculously hidden from his subordinates, and accepting as calmly as I could the role of punchbag for pent-up exasperation and anger. I would so much rather have been fighting beside my friends in command of a troop, as befitted my years, but this was no time for personal regrets.

Day by day our salient grew more compressed. The Franco-British attempt to counter-attack and close the gap had failed. Held back frontally by British regular troops, who never throughout the whole retreat were forced directly by Germans out of a position, Hitler's armies closed in behind us on flanks held by weak territorial and French divisions in the south, and by Belgians in the north. Early one morning as we stood beside our tanks in chilly rain, the final blow fell. Belgium had capitulated and the BEF was to be evacuated by the one port left open to us: Dunkirk.

All transport vehicles except those needed to carry men, and all kit, were to be smashed up and left, not burnt. We were to start for Dunkirk at once. Outmanœuvred, defeated and, as we then thought, disgraced, we were to be bundled unceremoniously back to England; there was to be no Marne, no counter-attack; where our fathers had succeeded, their sons had failed. We experienced, first, a sense of bitter shame—then more practically we looked at a map and wondered what the chances of reaching England in fact were. We were some miles further away from Dunkirk than the Germans, then besieging Calais.

All clothing, kit and impedimenta that could not conveniently be carried on our tanks was dumped in ponds and ditches, and we were on our way to the coast. Congestion on the roads steadily increased. A very large number of units had merely been given the order "Go to Dunkirk"; there was no control or order in the columns, which simply forced themselves on to the roads and drove down them. Soon there was utter chaos. Columns tried to pass one another and got jammed in the darkness. Ahead a dull red glow appeared; Dunkirk was on fire. On the left flank, and apparently not at all far away, German infantry flares rose and fell. Dawn broke to find our column split up irretrievably amongst others, and brought to a halt by a solid line of lorries from rear administrative units.

Exasperated, several of us went forward to try to get the column moving again. To our fury and dismay we discovered that these lorries were deserted, some with engines still running, left by their drivers to their fate. One by one we drove and manhandled them into a ditch and cleared the road. A little further on was another column of lorries in the same condition; this time they were French. All that was needed to complete this despicable scene of terror and confusion was a few German bombers, but these miraculously, and mercifully, did not materialise.

We struggled painfully and angrily forward. Approaching Dunkirk, the road became wider and we pushed on down it. On both sides stood hundreds of abandoned lorries filled with every conceivable form of military supplies—worth millions. This, we thought grimly, must be the most disgraceful rout in British military history; we felt we could hardly show our faces in England even in the somewhat unlikely event of our getting there. Dunkirk itself presented a most discouraging appearance, ruined, burning, and shrouded for much of the time in thick oily smoke from a smouldering refinery. We halted in an insalubrious brickyard and awaited reports from the beaches.

When they came it was clear that the chaos on the roads had been extended to the water's edge. The Embarkation Staff had been knocked out by a bomb, and nobody at that stage was in control. There was a vast mob of disorganised soldiery on the beaches, many with neither officers nor arms, their only instructions "embark at once"; this order, but no other, they had every intention of obeying with all speed and with minimum consideration for others. This concourse was being steadily bombed by the Germans and the din and confusion were of shattering proportions.

To be fair, this was the worst moment of the evacuation. Shortly after this a few strong-minded and vigorous personalities took control of embarkation and sorted out much of the bedlam. The soldiers on the beaches, and the drivers of the abandoned vehicles lining the roads, were mostly soldiers in name only, called up for the administrative services from civilian life shortly before, badly trained and officered; their discipline had long since, and hardly surprisingly, disintegrated. Nevertheless, I have always been surprised at the shining halo with which the so-called Dunkirk veterans have since been invested. No praise can be too high for the regulars who devotedly and bloodily held the ring while the main bodies withdrew behind them, but they were in a minority; the rest have very little indeed to be proud of.

All that night Dunkirk rocked under the crash and thunder of bombs. We woke to the news that the situation on the beaches was improving and that we might embark that day. Soon after, this was altered and we moved out to help the two divisions which had been ordered to hold out until either the evacuation was completed or they were overwhelmed, whichever was the sooner. We were told privately at regimental headquarters that there was now in fact little chance of us ever embarking at all. We were, however, beyond believing our own eyes by that time, still less what anybody told us, and we took this depressing news in our stride.

We spread ourselves out among the infantry along the network of canals and dykes which protect Dunkirk. Soon German infantry closed in all round the bridgehead, but the tanks, it was learnt much later, had been halted by Hitler because of the unsuitability of the ground. The bombers raided the beaches and left us alone. Two days passed, and with the departure of the majority of the BEF, the clutter and confusion became noticeably less. Surprisingly, the Germans did not make much progress, though as more troops left the thinner became the line and the more frequent the crises.

By the morning of June 1st, however, the situation became critical. The German attacks grew more and more violent and we were forced to put in two counter-attacks which cost us several men. The incredible good fortune of fine weather and flat calm throughout the evacuation had given rise to reasonable hopes of completing the whole re-embarkation within twenty-four hours. In fact, it looked as if those who were not embarked that night would be left behind, for the Navy doubted whether on the following night ships would be able to return.

After a hectic day we began to withdraw to the beaches as darkness fell. At one o'clock in the morning regimental headquarters arrived at the water's edge. Here we spiked our guns, smashed up the engines and abandoned, not without a pang, the tanks which had rumbled so proudly out of Colchester nine months before.

The beach was crowded with British and French soldiers —fit, wounded, dying and dead. But now there was no fuss; these were real soldiers. For hour after hour they had waited uncomplainingly, some in great pain, for their turn to wade out to sea to the waiting boats. All had their arms; their discipline held as firmly as it had done throughout their whole tragic, gallant retreat. Out in the dark expanse of sea we heard the splash of oars and cheerful British voices.

The evacuation from Dunkirk, irrespective of what had gone before, was a deliverance so improbable and unexpected that it must truly rank as a miracle. The rescue of the entire BEF together with many thousands of French troops, a high proportion of the force in a defenceless condition, through a small port closely invested by the enemy for a week and under heavy bombing for longer, was an incredible feat. The Royal Navy, the RAF, the regular troops, and the crews of myriad small craft to whom belongs the credit could never have performed it without two circumstances beyond Allied control. The first was the heaven-sent weather, the second was Hitler's decision, taken for reasons which have never been entirely clear, not to press home his attacks on the beach-head.

In that beleaguered BEF were the flower and indispensable cadres of Britain's regular Army, without which future expansion on an adequate scale would have been impossible. In that Army were serving almost all Britain's wartime military leaders, Alanbrooke, Alexander, Montgomery, Horrocks, Dempsey, Anderson and many more. I repeat, its survival was a miracle, and it is my firm belief that through this deliverance Hitler lost the war.

All these fine thoughts were well beyond my ken, or indeed my interest, as I collapsed in an exhausted sleep on the deck of a destroyer. When I woke it was daylight, and I saw we were at Harwich. There was a large crowd of people on the quayside. Somewhat to my surprise they were not booing us or throwing rotten eggs. In fact they were cheering—most odd.

CHAPTER THREE

Tank Battle

FOR many soldiers, of whom I was one, the return from Dunkirk marked the beginning of a thoroughly frustrating period—the long, slow trudge towards the Second Front. It was lucky for our peace of mind that we did not know how long, nor how dreary, this period of inactivity was to be.

The dramatic summer of 1940 centred our thoughts round invasion, on defence. Events in the Middle East, and the improvement in our defences at home, soon began to swing our minds and hopes back to overseas adventures. A great Army, as yet pathetically under-equipped, was beginning to take shape in the home base, and it was clear that this was not intended entirely for home defence.

New armoured regiments were being raised, civilian regiments based on a small regular cadre but otherwise starting entirely from scratch. I suddenly found myself, in 1941, a Major commanding a squadron in one of these regiments, the 23rd Hussars. The military history books told us that this title had once before graced a regiment of the British Army, but that in the Peninsular War the Duke of Wellington had disbanded the unit for immorality. When, in 1946, the reincarnation of this Peninsular casualty was in its turn disbanded, it was for more honourable reasons.

In 1941 the 23rd Hussars was merely somebody's brain-child, a collection of individuals with very little in common. Most of these individuals, but certainly not all, were from the north of England. Age and social groups varied wildly; so did trades. A few had been soldiers before, but for the vast majority the Army was something totally strange, a sort of joke which nobody took seriously till war began and then viewed with humorous resignation. To them, regular officers and, particularly, Sergeant-majors were no more than types imitated to good effect by films and the radio. Having never before met any of the types in person, these good but unmilitary citizens regarded them as simply one more inconvenience, a rather ludicrous one, amongst the many which the war was inflicting upon them. Several of these recruits were middle-aged and responsible, owners of small businesses and accustomed to being treated with respect; others, though younger, had minds and views of their own which did not by any means run on military lines. They were not bolshy, just independent.

The 23rd Hussars began with no tradition, except the unfortunate one already referred to and which we success-fully forgot. They were not even an offshoot of any par-ticular regular regiment and thus able to inherit, so to speak, a tradition secondhand. They had no territorial ties or basis. The regiment was simply the product of some-body's signature at the War Office. From this fountainhead it sprang like Minerva, though—unlike her—totally un-armed; indeed cloth caps and baggy grey trousers were its uniform for many days.

Since I served with the 23rd Hussars I have often wondered—blasphemously for a regular soldier—whether we do not get too excited about the effect tradition has on regimental spirit and will to fight. Everyone worth con-sidering is loyal to his regiment, particularly that in which he fought, but any reasonably intelligent person can assess at the end of a campaign what his own and other regiments are really worth, even if he never admits it. I can only say that in the bitter and severe north Europe campaign this collection of civilians, with no tradition or regimental background, despite very heavy casualties and the most trying circumstances, achieved for the 23rd Hussars a reputation only shared by two or three other armoured regiments at the most, regular or territorial. I know this to be so. Their morale and spirit remained throughout undimmed, and despite disbandment still endures in post-war comradeship in a way not excelled, and sometimes not equalled, by thriving regular regiments. Thus, when I am told now, as I frequently am, that traditions and past regimental glories are indispensable to morale and fighting spirit, I think of the 23rd Hussars and wonder.

Much of the credit for the regiment's success must go to our Colonel, Perry Harding, whose impact on this civilian army was immediate and favourable. He possessed not only personality, but had, as one of the foremost amateur jockeys of this or any era, spent so much time in the immediate pre-war years in non-military circles that he in no way, in appearance or conversation, conformed to anyone's idea of a stage Colonel. He was extremely tough, and his method of address was racy, in more senses than one. His character provoked amongst his command a healthy degree of alarm combined with amusement—a very effective combination.

The rest of our very small regular cadre, less experienced in the ways of these civilian soldiers, at first found it uphill work. The time-honoured methods of rapping out orders and then shouting if they were not satisfactorily obeyed proved a complete failure when I tried them in my squadron. The keen young regular, as yet blinkered, found his clear-cut, well-tried, orthodox methods muffled in a sort of cottonwool created mainly by the reaction: "Who the hell does he think he is, ordering us around?" The person I was really sorry for was my poor batman, Ward, who had most loyally and in great spiritual pain volunteered to leave his beloved Inniskillings and accompany me into this new and, he suspected, inferior world. Now he found himself a hostage, the target for all the rude remarks which my squadron did not dare address to me direct, and very unhappy he became.

After a few months, however, enough of what was good and sensible on both sides had rubbed off on each other. The squadron, somewhat to its secretly gratified surprise, had become quite military, and I had learnt a great deal, too. My officers had contributed much, unwittingly, to my education, for they were as variegated as the men—and just as entertaining. With Bunny Jones who sold sparking-plugs, and Bob Clark who sold barley, were Peter Walter, then an actor and now a manager, Jock Addison, now a well-known composer, and Felix Hookham—Margot Fonteyn's brother. To my squadron later came Bill Shebbeare and his wife Norma; their politics were so far to the Left that it became embarrassing to press them too hard on the subject, but their wit, their happy acceptance of their odd new surroundings, coupled with his enthusiasm which verged on the fanatical, made them engaging and attractive personalities. This company took me some way from the conversation of the pre-war cavalry mess.

The 23rd Hussars was one of the tank regiments in the newly formed Eleventh Armoured Division. This formation, later to earn a great fighting reputation in north-west Europe, was commanded in its early days by a formidable personality. General Percy Hobart had been a tank pioneer, one of the progressives thrown up by the Tank Corps in its early days of struggle. In the first months of the war he had spoken his mind once too often and had been sent home from the Western Desert to retirement and the post of Lance-Corporal in the Home Guard. Mr Churchill had not only extracted him from the Home Guard but had appointed him to raise and command an armoured division, which, with spirits and confidence in no way dampened by his vicissitudes, the General vigorously proceeded to do.

His divisional sign was a black and charging bull, and that was exactly how this most alarming General appeared to us. He had an abrupt, rapid way of addressing subordinates, and he made it obvious that behind his quickfire questions and intimidating mien a powerful and decisive brain was estimating whether or not you were up to your job. Here was a General whose bark was quite bad enough, but whose bite broke the usual rule by being far worse. If he decided that an officer must go, the officer went that day. The decision was taken on what many people might think was inadequate evidence, but the Bull considered him wanting and that was enough. After one manœuvre his "bag" was alleged to be one Brigadier, three Commanding Officers and five Majors; this was admittedly a record but not by much. Languid cavalry officers were like a red rag to this Bull and it was surprising how quickly all signs of languor dropped from those members of the small regular cadres who survived the first few months of the Eleventh Armoured Division's existence.

The soldiers, of course, thought the Bull was wonderful. Here was a General who dressed rather like they did and who obviously cared as little for spit and polish. He did not go in for polished riding-boots and shining brass; clad in black beret and battledress he was forever poking about the tank park, addressing the tank crews in a fatherly fashion and obviously terrifying the officers in a way most satisfactory to behold. His creed was work, and yet more work, in the tank park, at our tactics, till seven in the evening every day, Sundays included; he drove and inspired this army of civilians by force of a personality which, as we progressed towards his goal, showed increasing signs of humanity behind the iron front.

His leadership, hard and unrelenting as it was, exactly struck the mood of the times. Other divisions, as I knew from experience, were still working at peacetime pressure only slightly stepped up; life in the Eleventh Armoured reflected the urgency and drama of the military situation. Our officers and soldiers had not left their families and jobs at personal sacrifice in order to idle about in some unattractive military camp; they wanted to feel that they were contributing towards national survival. In this Division, and in the 23rd Hussars, there very soon grew out of this intensity of work a feeling of corporate affection and loyalty which made us all feel proud, in a way which few would have believed possible some months before, of our squadron and regiment—of our mob, as the soldiers called it. The pride lay in positive achievement, for here, where once was nothing, was now a regiment rapidly becoming fit to fight. Time had not been wasted; personal sacrifice had not gone unrewarded.

By the beginning of 1942 we had trained so hard and intensively that we considered ourselves ready for battle. In fact we were not ready, but then no regiment ever really is; there are always finishing touches that can be added. We could in fact have held our own quite adequately on the battlefield, and in our new-found confidence and sense of achievement there seemed no task which we could not master then and there. The Western Desert must surely claim us soon, if not the Second Front in Europe, for which the Russians were already clamouring and which American strength would soon make possible. The real facts of wartime life were mercifully hidden from us. In the two years which were to pass before the 23rd Hussars saw action only one conviction held together our morale and spirit; that action was just around the corner. Merciful ignorance indeed. Even so this was a hard and, for many of us, agonising period.

It is sometimes forgotten that a very large part of the British Army passed the middle war years in the role of lookers-on. The newspapers and the radio told us daily of desperate losing battles in Libya, the Far East and in Russia. We sat, members of a trained regiment, safe in England and heard of disaster after disaster; we read the casualty lists and talked to friends who had been in the thick of it. We visited London, then despite the blitz enjoying a boom in theatrical and night-club life, and there were the RAF officers, beribboned and fresh from action in German and British skies. Our sense of unreasonable but understandable inferiority deepened with mounting frustration. We officers could never show this feeling in front of our men, for already I spent much time in trying to prevent the more adventurous spirits from volunteering for scenes of action. "Your time to fight will come soon enough," I would say with a confidence which I did not feel, "and then it's best to go in with your friends—hang on a bit longer." And I would send the adventurous one away, wondering if I was doing right and whether it was not time for me to follow his example and take what was the easy way out. For it was so easy to volunteer and swan irresponsibly off to fight on some unknown field; so hard to sit it out and hope. For reasons, possibly mistaken, of loyalty I did not try to leave the 23rd Hussars; for better or worse, I decided to see them, and the squadron which was my creation, through to the end.

The invasion of French North Africa provided us with a sudden and thrilling uplift of spirits. News came through that the Eleventh Armoured Division had been selected, over the heads of at least one division senior to it, to reinforce our invading forces. The regiment's sixty tanks were prepared for embarkation at record speed and set off by train to the port. I led the wheeled vehicles northwards, similarly prepared. We were all in a high state of exhilaration; goodbye letters had been written and farewells were behind us. As my column passed Doncaster race-course I was told the whole thing was off. An infantry division was to go instead. We came back, and our Brigadier tried to restore our morale by organising a gardening competition round our huts. Exercise Turnabout, as we bitterly named this abortive expedition, was over.

As the war swung towards the Allies, with the end of the North African campaign and the invasion of Italy, we became more and more alarmed that we would never see any action at all. Our gaze became fixed on what was now our final hope, the invasion of Europe. Here, at last, the omens seemed favourable.

We were re-equipped with the Sherman tank, which at the time of the battle of Alamein had proved itself superior to any German tank. The fact that this moment of superiority had long since passed was not noted at the time. Our commanders were replaced by desert veterans; the Bull had gone to fresh pastures. Our training was stepped up to a pitch which we had not endured since 1941, and Generals Eisenhower and Montgomery came to look us over. We were initiated into the mysteries of sealing tanks to enable them to wade through waves. The feeling grew that this time there would be no Exercise Turnabout.

Nor was there. In May, 1944, the division concentrated at Aldershot, and in an atmosphere of steadily mounting expectancy the news of D Day burst upon us. The Eleventh Armoured Division was to land after the assaulting troops and to provide part of the force which would subsequently break out and liberate France. We were soon on our way to Southampton and the landing-craft. We left behind us what was known as the "LOB" or left out of battle party, and to his fury Bill Shebbeare was put in charge of it. He had chafed more than any of us at our inactivity, and Exercise Turnabout had almost unhinged him; his hatred of Nazism was something far beyond anything which the rest of us, less politically minded, could feel. His dearest wish, as he wrote in his book *A Soldier Looks Ahead*, was to attack it—"this time not from a platform in a market-place or stool on a village green, but from the turret of a tank." Now his attack on it was delayed yet again, and he was very distressed indeed.

The rest of us assembled, as in a dream, in a Normandy of woods, small enclosed pastures, battered grey villages, and inhabitants not at all pleased to be liberated. It was immediately clear that the war was far from ended and that there was plenty of fighting still to be done. The casualties among the assaulting divisions had been heavy,

and the beach-head, despite the troops which were flowing
steadily into it, was little bigger than on the second day
of the invasion. There began a series of operations designed
to enlarge the beach-head, and to give the liberating armies
more elbow-room to prepare for the big break-out into
France. In one of these operations the 23rd Hussars had
their first taste of action.

In the thick *bocage* country this battle necessarily
centred round the infantry, with the armour in support. It
was scrappy, bloody and violent; it lasted, hammer and
tongs, for five days and gained us a little ground at considerable cost to our infantry. Our own casualties were not
light, although our part was secondary, and the battle provided the 23rd Hussars with a much-needed dose of realism
and experience.

Anxious as those five days had been, and sad though I
was at the loss of Bob Clark, the seller of barley, and other
friends, I felt pride in the way the squadron had come
through the test. As I walked among the crews on the day
after we were pulled out of the battle, their normal manner
of humorous efficiency was touched with an almost arrogant
self-confidence. At last they had justified themselves; they
had shown they could fight as well or better than regular
troops; their training had worked; the leadership and team-
work were proved in the fire of battle. They were real
soldiers at last. Their morale positively glowed, and as I
moved from crew to crew I warmed myself at its light. For
three years I had waited for this moment, and now after all
the doubt and uncertainty I felt that there was nothing
that my squadron could not do. I was, moreover, by this
time under no illusion that much remained to be done,
and I told them so.

I was sitting later that day having tea with my crew in
the trench we had dug next to our tank for protection
against shell-fire. We had all been together for years by this
time. Sam English, a tough and combative London bus-
driver, was brewing the tea; my two gunners, McGrath, a

cheerful Liverpudlian, and Ward, who had forsaken the chores of batman for a more active role, were assisting him in this ritual, the most important of the day. Sergeant Horrobin, my wireless operator, was watching them in his withdrawn and dignified way. He was one of the most efficient men I have ever met—almost frighteningly so; his brain worked like lightning and nothing ever seemed to throw him off balance. Whatever the tension and drama, he could be relied upon, with a quiet sentence or two to calm me by producing exactly what was required. He would make the most perfect secretary, I often thought. He was chatting quietly to me in his slow Yorkshire speech when a despatch-rider rode up from regimental headquarters and handed me a message. I read it, and the bottom of my world fell out. I was to hand over my squadron to Bill Shebbeare and report to headquarters as second-in-command of the regiment.

We sat in silence for several minutes. I think my crew were nearly as upset as I was. I could not imagine a greater anti-climax, to give up my active command at this of all moments, in order to sit at regimental headquarters as the number two. In war, however, you go where you are told, and in war, when unfortunate things are apt to happen to commanding officers, number two's are necessary. I rose to my feet and walked miserably round the squadron to say goodbye.

Bill Shebbeare had missed our first battle and had arrived only a day or so before with his LOB contingent. He had sprung—armed to the teeth—from the truck which brought him, with an air of expecting a Nazi to bounce out on him from behind the nearest bush. Now his luck had changed, and into his eager hand was placed the weapon which I had forged. I still treasure a note which that generous and brilliant little man penned to me that evening, and which I received sitting sadly in my strange new surroundings. "I do indeed believe C Squadron to be," he wrote, "the best armoured squadron in the Army, and everything I have seen of the men's spirit here confirms me in this. It makes me feel such a usurper to have taken over, ready made and without any effort on my own part, a squadron which you have taken three years to create. I feel when we go into action again that I need have no worries— except about my own ability to give them the leadership they deserve." He concluded, "I have always looked forward and still do to taking part in this campaign of liberation; but it never occurred to me that I should play a part so responsible and full of opportunity as leading C Squadron. If I have any success I shall owe it all to you, and the spirit you have created here."

Over now to Chester Wilmot, who was also observing the scene, albeit from a rather higher level. In his *Struggle for Europe* he writes: "By July 10th the situation in Normandy appeared to have reached a crisis. The American breakout offensive had bogged down. The enemy in the eastern half of Caen blocked the way to the Falaise plain. German infantry reinforcements from southern France were now reaching Normandy in a steady flow. Cherbourg harbour was not yet open, and only one Mulberry was working. The Allied Air Forces, handicapped by persistent bad weather over their English bases, were disgruntled because Second Army had not yet captured the Caen airfields. At SHAEF Tedder and Morgan were openly critical of Montgomery's conduct of the battle, and there were murmurs against him in Whitehall, where the Jeremiahs were already predicting a stalemate. Across the Atlantic the American press was impatient and the US War Department was beginning to voice its concern at the slow development of operations.

"Even Eisenhower was affected by this uneasiness. Three days earlier he had written to Montgomery expressing the fear that the bridgehead was in danger of being sealed off, and urging him to launch and maintain an all-out offensive . . .

"Within the past ten days four German infantry divisions had reached Normandy, and three of these had been put into the line opposite the British, thus relieving Panzer formations which had begun moving to the American front. At all costs this westward movement had to be halted by a swift, bold stroke which would establish British armour on Bourguebus Ridge, south of Caen, and thus re-establish the menace of an imminent and powerful breakout towards Paris.

"The only possibility was to strike from the 'airborne bridgehead' east of the Orne. But this area offered so little room for assembly and so narrow a frontage for attack that a conventional operation was certain to be stopped long before infantry could cover the eight miles to Bourguebus Ridge. Accordingly Montgomery and Dempsey devised a revolutionary plan. They would group the three British armoured divisions under O'Connor's 8th Corps and send them roaring out of the Orne bridgehead behind an aerial bombardment of unprecedented ferocity."

The early Normandy battles had exploded the theory that the Sherman tank was any longer a match for the German Panzers. Since El Alamein the Germans had produced, on a large scale, the Tiger and the Panther tanks, mounting high velocity 88 and 75 millimetre guns which could drill a Sherman at two thousand yards. Moreover their frontal armour was impenetrable to the Sherman 75 millimetre gun at any range. At the last moment, and with improvisation which must have had incalculable consequences, the War Office had issued each armoured regiment, on a basis of one for every four tanks, with a Sherman mounting a seventeen-pounder gun. On this weapon, and often on this alone, depended the result of many an armoured engagement in Normandy. In other respects the British armoured formations relied on numerical superiority rather than on quality. This superiority was considerable. We heard on good authority that the number

of reserve Shermans was so great, and the number of infantry reserves so low, that armour had become expendable.
Whatever the tactical position in the bridgehead, it was
now imperative to use the armour *en masse*, in one supreme
effort, and regardless of casualties.

The result was Operation Goodwood. In great secrecy,
the three armoured divisions—Seventh, Eleventh and
Guards—were to be concentrated during the night of
July 17th, 1944, east of the Orne river, north-east of Caen.
Then, at first light on the 18th, preceded by an air and
artillery programme of huge proportions, the armour was
to be launched as a battering-ram. The Eleventh Armoured
Division was to lead, with their objective the Bourguebus
Ridge, eight miles from the start-line. The Guards and the
Seventh Armoured, the Desert Rats, were to follow and
exploit the gains of the Eleventh.

This vast assaulting force had, on its way to the start-line,
and subject to a tight timetable conforming to the requirements of Bomber Command, to cross a narrow bridge over
the Orne and negotiate one of our minefields which had
but three lanes cleared through it. It then had to shake out
and advance as close as possible behind the carpet of bombs
and the artillery barrage. There were two railway lines to
cross, and the air photographs did not encourage us to
think that this would be particularly easy, even with tanks.
Beyond the second railway line, with some three miles still
left to cover before the Bourguebus Ridge, our heavy artillery, unable to cross the bridge owing to the passage of the
three armoured divisions, would be out of range.

Our orders, despite these hazards, were at all costs to
keep going. The three divisions were to advance down a
narrow corridor which, initially at any rate, offered no
room for manœuvre. Regiments were to move in box formation, with all infantry and artillery vehicles within the box,
and with thirty yards between tanks. Our flanks, later to be
cleared by slower-moving infantry divisions, were to be
ignored. It was hoped that the bombing and artillery, im-

mediately followed by the impact of a mass of armour, would so demoralise and bludgeon the enemy that, before they could recover, the Bourguebus Ridge would be ours.

South of the Orne the open cornfields sloped gently down to the railway lines which we had studied on air photographs with such concern. Then the ground rose gradually to the Bourguebus Ridge, which dominated the corridor down which we were to advance. Between the suburbs of Caen to the west and the woods to the east of this corridor, an area some fifteen hundred yards wide, the plain was dappled with small villages. There were few hedgerows, no *bocage*; here, for the first time in the campaign, was country over which tanks could move. But the villages provided ideal and mutually supporting strongholds for enemy tanks and infantry, overlooked always by the dominating ridge for which we were aiming.

The part of the enemy front on which the assault was due to fall was the most sensitive and hence the strongest in the whole of Normandy. It protected not only the Caen airfields but the open plains over which British armour could shake itself free of the *bocage* and swarm across country and towards Paris. Our Intelligence estimated, optimistically as it turned out, that the enemy defences were some four miles deep, and that perhaps two Panzer divisions were held back behind the ridge in reserve. The more we studied the plan, the more we realised that all depended on our ability to follow at speed immediately behind the bombers and artillery. If we were to be delayed, and lose them, a host of unattractive possibilities loomed.

During the nights of the 16th and 17th July the Normandy beach-head reverberated with the roar and rattle of hundreds of tanks moving across to the eastern flank. By dawn on the 18th, the whole of Eleventh Armoured Division was to cross the Orne bridge and cram itself into the comparatively small area between the bridge and the start-line. The other armoured divisions could not begin

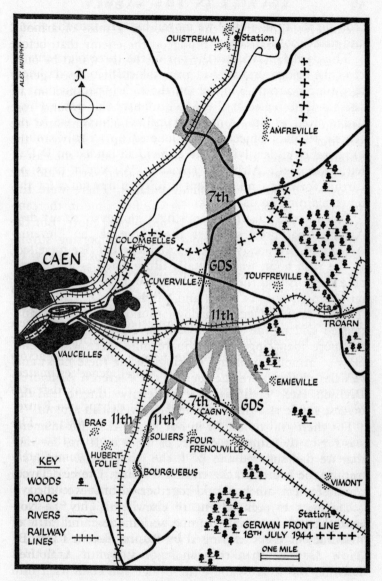

ALEX MURPHY

N

OUISTREHAM ● Station

AMFREVILLE

7th

COLOMBELLES

GDS

CAEN

CUVERVILLE

TOUFFREVILLE

Sta.

11th

TROARN

VAUCELLES

EMIEVILLE

7th GDS

CAGNY

BRAS 11th 11th

SOLIERS

FOUR
FRENOUVILLE

HUBERT-
FOLIE

BOURGUEBUS

VIMONT

KEY

WOODS ♣

ROADS ▬▬▬

RIVERS

RAILWAY
LINES ┼┼┼

Station
GERMAN FRONT LINE
18ᵀᴴ JULY 1944 ┼┼┼┼

ONE MILE

Operation Goodwood

crossing the bridge until we moved forward into the attack and made room for them.

The 23rd Hussars was the last of the three regiments to cross the bridge, and we had great difficulty in the darkness in pushing ourselves in behind the tightly-packed mass of tanks, self-propelled artillery and infantry half-tracks which had arrived earlier. Amongst familiar vehicles we found grotesque black objects which loomed up weirdly around us; derelict gliders lying where they had landed on D Day with the Sixth Airborne Division. We could press no further forward, and we slept fitfully in our tanks for the few remaining hours of darkness.

Dawn broke mistily, promising a gloriously sunny day. As the light grew stronger the whole of the Eleventh Armoured Division, vehicles packed together like travellers in the rush hour, was gradually illuminated as if grouped on a stage. But as the sun broke through the mist, glinting on the periscopes of tanks and windscreens of half-tracks, its rays casting jagged shadows round the smashed and twisted gliders, the stage illusion gave place to something far more menacing. For a square mile there was a solid mass of armour, pent up, waiting. Inside these tanks and vehicles of war were the men of the Eleventh Armoured Division, lately civilians, now soldiers; waiting to lead the biggest single assault ever launched by British armour.

For there was no doubt in our minds that this moment was for us the supreme climax of the war. It was for this that we had suffered the Bull, the years of toil and frustration, the boredom, the endless training, Exercise Turnabout; for this we had held together when it would have been easier to seek adventure elsewhere. The full-scale breakthrough into Nazi Europe, so long despaired of, was at hand; our mood expressed by Rupert Brooke's words: "Now, God be thanked who has matched us with His hour."

The mist dissolved and the sun grew stronger. Our ears strained for the sound of the bombers, our eyes scanned the smiling Normandy countryside over which we were to advance. Peacefully it lay; not a sign of the enemy was visible in the cornfields or amongst the grey villages; not a move, surprisingly, indicated that the enemy had either seen or resented the arrival of an enormous mass of British armour during the night. The sunlit plain unrolled placidly before us in the most unwarlike fashion possible, and I thought of a patient lying unconscious beneath a surgeon's knife.

From the turrets of several tanks, arms pointed suddenly skywards. In an instant every head turned to gaze back behind us. In the dim distance, high over the Channel hung an almost indistinguishable dot. A distant beelike drone. Here came, from English bases, the entire British Bomber Command. As if an invisible hand was pulling a thread of black cotton from a reel hidden below the horizon, the great black Lancasters came slowly, one behind another, into our view; hundreds upon hundreds of them, streaming ponderously towards us, filling the air with the throb of their engines. High above them escorting Spitfires twisted and rolled, like silver fish in a blue translucent sea. This vast armada passed over our awed heads, contemptuous of opposition and apparently unscathed.

Before our eyes the quiet panorama over which we had recently gazed erupted suddenly into swirls of grey and brown dust, convulsed like a boiling cauldron. With a drumming, thudding roar the bombs obliterated it bit by bit from view, until there was nothing left to see but whirling, agitated dust punctuated by violent flashes. To us, about to fight our way forward through a formidable enemy position, this dramatic overture was like strong brandy. We stood up in our tanks and waved and cheered. Still the Lancasters came, now interspersed with smaller medium bombers, an unimaginable number of bombers, raining destruction down on the now-invisible country before us. For an hour or more, and growing fainter as more distant targets were attacked, this punishment continued.

The last aircraft turned for home but the air was still throbbing and thudding with explosions. Six hundred guns had taken over. Soon the rolling barrage would begin. Then it would be our turn. All round me the crews were settling down into their turrets, adjusting their helmets and headsets, commanders shuffling with their mapboards, and telling their drivers to start up. I looked back. Just behind regimental headquarters was my late squadron, and my late tank. Sam English was just closing down his driver's hatch, and gave me a parting grin as he disappeared from view; Bill Shebbeare, unrecognisable beneath helmet and goggles, returned my wave cheerfully. Before us the two leading regiments, the 3rd Royal Tanks and the Fife and Forfar Yeomanry, were beginning to move, clouds of dust were rising as the Shermans revved up their engines, and the medley of self-propelled guns, half-tracks, scout cars, ambulances, jolted and jerked forwards behind them.

Thrilling as this densely packed mass of armour appeared as it rumbled forward into battle, I could not stifle a feeling of misgiving. How on earth, I wondered, were all those vehicles going to keep up with the tanks, through a minefield, across cratered country? If they got left behind, as they undoubtedly would, they would hold back the regiments behind them. How then would we maintain the tight formation and the impetus so necessary to carry us forward before the shock of bombardment had worn off? And how long would the following armoured divisions, still on the wrong side of the Orne, take to catch up? But we were launched now, and there was nothing to be done but press forward and hope.

The entrances to the minefield were clearly marked with white tape and, despite the haze of dust and cordite, easy to find. The lanes were narrow, and we had to pass down them in single file. Meanwhile the leading tanks were keeping up with the barrage, and behind them

straggled their supporting vehicles. Instead of advancing
three hundred yards in rear of the regiment in front of us,
we crossed the start-line at least a mile behind it.

The open country over which we were motoring was
flanked on each side by woods which had been heavily
bombed. Infantry divisions were working through them
but clearly could not be expected to go as fast as we could
drive across the cornfields. Our flanks would therefore be
exposed to such enemy as had survived the bombardment.
We went forward with guns traversed outwards and our
gaze searching the battered woods lining our corridor. For
three miles, however, we roared unhindered and un-
opposed into enemy country, past smoking villages and
devastated farms. German soldiers, white and semi-con-
scious, staggered past us on their way to our lines. Many
more crouched stunned, terrified, and in some cases
literally drunk, in dug-outs as we passed, to be winkled out
by infantry later.

The embankment of the first railway line had proved
easily passable for tanks, but when we arrived there an unhappy gaggle of infantry half-tracks and wheeled vehicles
was queueing up for the gaps which engineers had blown
for them. By the time the 23rd Hussars were across, the
two leading regiments had disappeared from view, and we
received an order from Brigade Headquarters to watch for
a counter-attack by Tigers on our left flank. No sooner had
this order been received than a Sherman of one of our
leading squadrons went up in flames about two hundred
yards in front of me.

There can be few greater shocks to the senses than the
sight, at close quarters, of a tank struck by armour-piercing
fire. As the heavy solid shell hits and penetrates the armour
plate there is an intense explosion and a blinding white
flash, as if the tank had been hit by lightning. Bits of metal
and equipment, flying violently outwards, are silhouetted
blackly and instantaneously against the flash. A pause,
smoke and flames wreathe upwards out of the turret, frantic

figures leap or crawl painfully out on to the hull and drop, clothing probably on fire, to earth. Then with a rush and a crackle the fire takes hold, flames wreathe upwards out of the turret and then with vivid flashes the ammunition begins to explode. A few hours later all that remains is a black, smouldering hulk.

When hit, the Sherman was, as the tank men called it, a quick "brewer". It gave the occupants very little time indeed to bale out before it burst into flames; the ammunition was exposed within the turret, and, it was believed, became ignited by the energy created by the concussion. Other types of tanks allowed a much more gentlemanly interval for evacuation. It was hard, therefore, always to pull the wounded out of a Sherman in time, and from the crew of five we used to average, for every tank knocked out, one man untouched, two wounded but safe, and two who failed to emerge.

The stricken tank in front of me caused our guns to traverse as one towards the direction from which the fire had come. There was a wood away to our left and amongst the trees two dark, low shapes which crawled and spat. We fired and manœuvred against them for a while, until the first tanks of the Guards Armoured Division came behind us. Then we were ordered to hand the Tigers over to the Guards and hurry forward to receive fresh orders from Brigade Headquarters.

Brigadier Roscoe Harvey sat on the edge of his tank looking no more concerned than he had on that far away day at Aldershot when Rareweed and I had deadheated with him. "I can't make out what's happened to the Fifes," he said. "They're obviously having the hell of a battle but we can't raise them on the air at all now. The 3rd Tanks are on their right and the last I heard from them was that they were going well for Bourguebus Ridge. I want the 23rd Hussars to pass through the Fife and Forfar and continue on up to the objective. Get going, we're behind schedule and our masters behind are in the devil of a hurry."

We surged forward again across the fields like a battle fleet, with white dust in our wake instead of spray. Astride the axis of our advance A and B Squadrons breasted the corn together, after them came the four tanks of our head-quarters, then C. The second railway line provided a small but easily passable embankment, and here we paused, field-glasses glinting from every turret as commanders examined the open ground sloping up to Bourguebus Ridge three miles away. It was littered with tanks, in the haze of smoke and mist impossible to identify as friend or foe, alive or dead. They were just sitting there. "The 3rd Tanks are supposed to be well forward," said Perry Harding to the leading squadrons. "Advance, and we'll find out from the Fifes what's happening. C Squadron stay here in reserve."

A mile further forward we reached the tail of the Fife and Forfars, who were sitting in the middle of the open plain beneath the ridge. There was about as much cover there as there is on a polo-field and nobody would sit there without good reason. Why were they so still? Suddenly we realised that all these tanks were dead, that the only signs of life came from blackened, dishevelled parties on foot, tending wounded and trickling to the rear. A scout car wound its way through the confusion to Perry's tank and from it, hatless and smoke-grimed, sprang John Gilmour, one of the Fife and Forfar squadron leaders. "I don't think we've got more than four tanks left in action," were his opening words, delivered in his usual calm and matter-of-fact way. "When we and the 3rd Tanks were just short of the ridge we got taken on by Panzers and guns from the top of it, and as you can see there's no cover, so I should watch out."

In front of us were two small hamlets, Soliers and Four, now reduced to piles of brick rubble among some drunken trees. From these two villages and from the woods lining the summit of Bourguebus Ridge there now came a violent attack upon us. Just as the Fifes and 3rd Tanks had been broken up by high velocity fire, so now we in our turn found ourselves lying at the bottom of a saucer being fired at from along at least half of the rim. The Shermans' seventy-fives were hopelessly outranged and ineffective, the seventeen-pounder tanks, conspicuous with their long gun and by now well-known to the Germans, were accorded top priority for destruction. B Squadron and then A Squadron, firing back furiously, began to lose tank after tank.

Perry Harding was down inside his Sherman when this onslaught began, engaged in urgent conversation with the Brigadier and quite unconscious of events outside. With a loud thump a fountain of earth shot up ten yards in front of his tank. It was time for regimental headquarters to go into action. My gunner, no less a personage than the Regimental-Sergeant-Major, slammed a long armour-piercing shell into the breech and remained gazing down the telescope sight awaiting my order. Amongst the derelict tanks littering the slope up to the ridge were crawling the unmistakeable shapes of Tigers and Panthers. One, a Panther, had its barrel pointing in our direction—indeed the tank was head on to me, presenting a sloping front too thick for my gun to penetrate. This was clearly the miscreant who had fired at Perry. "Traverse right, steady . . . on, six hundred . . . fire!" The blast buffeted my face as I peered at the target out of the turret, the recoil mechanism by my knee smacked back in its cradle, depositing the empty shell with a clatter on the floor. I was deaf and blind to all but the sight of my tracer projectile streaking towards its target. It struck exactly centrally, a shower of sparks and then, to my delighted astonishment, figures baling out; the shot must by great good fortune have hit the one vulnerable spot, the join between turret and hull. Perry was now aware of what was going on; we threw out smoke grenades to cover our slow withdrawal to an inadequate hedgerow a few hundred yards in rear, where the hectic, slogging battle continued. "Press on!"

were still the orders from behind. "Hurry. German reserves are rushing across from other parts of the front—press forward to the high ground before they arrive. The Guards and Seventh Armoured are delayed—you will get no help from them today. On, on!"

With the villages of Four and Soliers as yet untaken, and with the Bourguebus Ridge obviously well-stocked with German tanks and 88-millimetre anti-tank guns, this order, with our tank strength now gravely reduced, was unrealistic to say the least. But the stakes were high, and those behind must be excused for squeezing the last ounce of impetus from the holocaust they had unleashed that morning.

C Squadron, behind us and out of sight over a low ridge to our left, was now the last armoured reserve of the division. To its commander was communicated the full sense of the urgency and drama of the situation, the need for speed and, if necessary, for sacrifice. He was told to press forward through the village of Four.

It is so easy to be calm and dispassionate after a battle; to forget how you felt and thought at the time, amid the tumult, the stress, and the haze of smoke and dust. In a dogfight such as this armoured battle had become, clear descriptions of enemy positions and the exact relationship of the map to the ground became difficult if not impossible. Instructions over the wireless can seldom take the place of a personal meeting before an attack to clear up misunderstandings. But there was now no time for personal meetings, only rapid, dramatic instructions and acknowledgments over the air while C Squadron bumped forward across the pockmarked ground.

Bill Shebbeare, with the fire suppressed so long within him now bursting forth, and without the self-confidence born of battle experience, was in no mood for caution. A colder more experienced man might have looked harder before he leapt, have probed and prodded until he found a way through; but he would have needed much assurance thus to have temporised and to have defied the mood of the moment. This mood was for attack, violent, immediate attack, at whatever the cost.

C Squadron rolled forward towards the ruins of Four like a wave, and on the rocks of hidden guns and Panzers it was wrecked and broken. Simultaneously, like a row of torches ignited at a fiesta, the tanks of the three troops and squadron headquarters were hit and blazing. Dazed survivors ran to and fro, helping the wounded, beating out flaming clothing with their hands, until the heat and explosions drove them back out of the inferno which once had been fifteen battle tanks.

Out of sight over the low ridge our headquarters waited anxiously for progress reports. None came. No reply to our calls. Just as I was about to drive round and investigate, one of the surviving tank commanders succeeded in getting through on the air. Five tanks were left, and back where they had started. The squadron leader's tank had been destroyed, and so indeed had the whole of squadron headquarters. One of the troop officers was known to have been killed; Bunny Jones, Peter Walter, Jock Addison were all wounded. Later, as further messages came through, the toll rose and I realised that C Squadron had probably lost all its officers save one, and at least half of its NCO tank commanders. "How about the squadron leader and his crew?" I nerved myself to ask. "McGrath slightly wounded, English and Ward badly burnt but alive. No news of the rest of the crew." No news of Sergeant Horrobin, or of Bill Shebbeare. Both, we later learnt, were dead.

I went back to the regimental aid post. About a hundred wounded lay in the corn awaiting evacuation. Some of the more lightly wounded were gallantly forcing themselves to act as orderlies. Most of the others, terribly burnt and blackened, were making pathetic efforts to help and cheer each other. As they moved or were carried towards the waiting ambulances this tragic but indomitable assembly broke defiantly into song, chanting with cracked voices the same

The finish of the Aldershot Open Cup, 1937. Rareweed is nearest the camera.

(Above) One of our Shermans moves forward into battle.

Fencing in the British team at the World Modern Pentathlon Championship at Hälsingborg in 1951.

(Above) Ronnie Cronin going over the "Chair" in the Topham Trophy at Aintree, 1952.

(Below) Pointsman (left) was third at the last fence in the Grand Military Gold Cup at Sandown Park in 1954 but finally won by a neck.

ribaldries as they had sung together at concerts round the camp fires in happier days.

The attack to which they had given so much was for the time being at a standstill. On the slopes of Bourguebus Ridge were scattered the corpses of one hundred and six British tanks, and a considerable number of German tanks. The survivors of both sides hung dourly on to their gains, like exhausted boxers who know that they are too tired to land a knockout. Evening fell and with it the battle temporarily died, to the sound of artillery and the sight of a myriad flickering fires from the hulks littering the plain. Over it all hung the bitter smell of burning.

This battle, which continued inconclusively for two more days, was probably the biggest and the most intense ever fought by British armour. Almost certainly, with the advent of nuclear weapons, nothing like it will ever be seen again. It provoked much comment, mostly bitter, in military circles at the time, and arguments about it still simmer. General Montgomery said the battle had been a success; others equally exalted proclaimed it a failure. We did not much care which it was. We had for the first time seen war for the ugly and unfair monster that it is, all glamour stripped from it. Overnight we lost our crusading zeal and became professionals. Rupert Brooke's words were forgotten.

The 23rd Hussars recovered, and recovered very soon. New faces, new commanders and new crewmen filled the gaps. Within a week we were fighting hard again, with less abandon and with more wary eyes, but just as hard and just as well. And so it continued until the end. A regimental spirit must indeed be brittle if the shock of one serious reverse can crack it, and there was nothing brittle about our mob. Their spirit endured then, and endures still. A tradition is none the worse for being only four years old.

C

CHAPTER FOUR

Reflections on VE Day

IT was Victory-in-Europe Day, and we were celebrating. For the last three days, since our advance across Germany had been halted, we had had little to do but plan our revelry. Now, with the same thoroughness and enterprise which had won the regiment so many victories, we had all gone crazy.

Round the enormous bonfires piled high with broken German vehicles, crowds of men, bottles in hand, swayed and sang. Verey lights soared upwards; parachute flares descended, trying to emulate Brock. In the distance anti-aircraft guns fired a salute; in retaliation our sappers let off lumps of gelignite, whose thunderous explosions broke the local windows. Some of the more enterprising soldiers began to fire tank machine-guns into the air and to discharge smoke bombs for good measure. German lorries were driven headlong into the roaring bonfires, the driver leaping out as he neared the flames. And so it continued until dawn.

In fact, it was the flattest party ever. Very few people felt like it; we went through the motions because it seemed to be the right thing to do and eventually we lashed ourselves into a suitable degree of craziness. There was too much sorrow around us in the shape of the pathetic, cowed Germans and too much sorrow stored up in our hearts after six years of war. There was, too, the question: "What now?" For almost as long as we could remember we had been under strain, as if heaving on a rope, and suddenly the other end had collapsed. Nothing to pull against any more. This was it. The end of the war. Under the surface gaiety a flat, dead feeling, not exultation; uncertainty and aimlessness where all had been hard and purposeful.

Many of the men dancing and shouting round the bonfires had known no other adult existence save war. They had grown accustomed to this strange life in which personal liberty and initiative had been suspended for the duration, and they had almost ceased, except in terms of minor tactics, to think for themselves. They had never known the normal life of a young man in his twenties; they were tired, war-weary and strained, their strength drawn from and depending on their mutual comradeship and regimental loyalty. The mad rejoicings of VE Day were, in part, a paean of thankfulness for the end of an ordeal which they, somewhat unexpectedly, had been spared to see, in part reassurance for eyes that feared to look into the future.

The framework of life was about to be dismantled. Close friends, with nothing in common but shared regimental experiences, would be absorbed into the different walks of life ordained for them in pre-war days, and very soon become memories to each other, much as a favourite billet or an unpleasant battle were already wartime memories. The solid, clear-cut friendliness of the regimental fraternity would soon be a memory too, and its members be making their individual ways in a world at whose image they could now only guess. We had fought to reach this VE Day; it had been our goal for years and we were deeply thankful to have reached it; we were heartily sick of war but apprehensive, at heart, of peace.

I felt apprehension and also a sense of wasted time. I was nearly thirty and exclusively a soldier, having tasted none of the many interests which occupy young men at a time when their athletic powers, mental receptiveness and nerve are at their peak. I determined to make up for lost time, to include in this unseen world of peacetime soldiering all and more that I had missed of life outside my profession. Somehow, I would pay myself back those missing years.

The men who trickled back into civilisation from the watersheds of VE Day and VJ Day all had to pay themselves back those missing years. Some had to create or build up their jobs, others to catch up with a growing family. I was much luckier than most; soon to be, but not yet, married, and already some distance up the ladder of my profession. I could fumble my way into this odd peacetime world with the knowledge that my bread and butter was as safe as it had always been. It was now up to me to put the jam on it.

CHAPTER FIVE

A Ride at Aintree

BACK in England, it was hard at first to take an interest in theoretical soldiering after so much practical experience. It soon became apparent, however, that unless I took the theory, and the examinations which went with it, seriously, I should very soon drop out of the race and end up as an elderly and unpromoted officer posted to some unattractive and boring part of the world. This prospect by no means fitted in with my plans and I realised very quickly that the first essential was to do quite a lot of judiciously-timed work, while using my leisure to escape from the military world into a different, civilian, one.

I have thus lived, in varying degrees of intensity, a kind of double life ever since. The soldiering side has necessarily been my main preoccupation, with the other side, whatever it may have been, fitted into any gaps which appeared in the military edifice. Balancing these two lives has sometimes been a precarious business but there is nothing wrong with that.

My first "second life" was lived in the world of steeplechasing. This was natural, for I had ridden in many point-to-points in those far off days before the war, and in a few steeplechases. Perry Harding, one of the best amateur jockeys ever to ride, had been my Commanding Officer for four of the war years, and his stories of pre-war racing experiences had made me determined to try to emulate him.

I was not going to waste time paddling about in the shallows of point-to-point racing and I proceeded to jump in at the deep end as an amateur steeplechase jockey. Fortunately, I had saved up my pay during the war for just this moment and was able to buy a steeplechaser of my own. I thus avoided the alternative of letting it be known that there was no horse, however bad its jumping or unpleasant its habits, that I would not ride; a starting-point which was perfectly feasible though distinctly hazardous to life and limb.

When you know comparatively little about a new enterprise, it is best to put yourself in the hands of an expert. I had the luck, and for once the good sense, to place myself in the hands of Alec Kilpatrick, who trains at Collingbourne Ducis in Wiltshire. It was Alec who bought my first steeplechaser for me, who trained the horse, advised me, guided my footsteps, and generally played the part of candid friend. My new purchase was a little horse called September Air. He knew not much more about the game than I did, but his form was quite promising and he was a good if rather light-hearted jumper.

Our first venture together was at Nottingham and, not unexpectedly, I fell off—though not before we had had every prospect of otherwise finishing in the first three. Highly delighted, I rode him again, at Fontwell Park, and this time we were fourth. Then came the big freeze of 1947 and racing closed down till March. The thaw came only just in time for the Grand National Meeting.

I was determined to ride in the Grand National one day but this year, naturally, I was not entered, nor indeed was my horse qualified to run. There was, however, an opportunity of riding round part of the course, in one of the lesser steeplechases at the meeting, and this chance I seized. Since this was only our third race together (and, owing to the frost, the second one had been some two months earlier) this enterprise was foolhardy in the extreme—but ignorance is bliss.

Those whose experience of National Hunt fences has been restricted to a distant view from the stands, or to television, may perhaps have a false idea of their size. The width of each fence and its slope tend to make it look smaller than it really is. In fact, regulations permit no fence to be lower than four feet six inches except the water jump, which has to be not less than twelve feet wide. These are normal fences, and Aintree is far from normal. The average height there is four feet ten inches and some are five feet; all are extremely solid; many, particularly Becher's Brook, have disconcerting drops on the landing side; and in those days the fences were very upright. While inspecting this course before your first ride at Aintree, it is hard to keep the conversation going in the lighthearted and cheerful style desirable for the occasion.

On that chilly and fogbound afternoon in March, sixteen jockeys, of whom I was one, rode forth to contest the Stanley Chase, over one circuit of the National course. Cantering down to the start, I remember thinking how unkind it was that on my first appearance at Aintree the fog should make the already formidable fences look double their real size. But, once we started, the ordeal did not seem so bad as I feared; the first two obstacles were surmounted successfully, and we turned away down the long line of fences leading to Becher's, swallowed up, as far as the stands were concerned, by the fog.

But now the race really became quite exciting. As the cavalcade encountered each fence, it was as if a covey of partridges was passing over a line of accurate guns; a proportion would plunge violently to the earth whilst the survivors streamed anxiously on. The company was dwindling considerably and, filled with an altogether premature optimism, I advanced confidently upon the fence before Becher's. Perhaps I had communicated my misplaced optimism to September Air, for at this point he underestimated the height of the fence by a considerable margin and paid the inevitable penalty. Down we went.

We hit the ground hard; it had seemed a long drop. My horse got up and galloped senselessly off into the fog. I rose, somewhat crestfallen and rather sore. Loose horses were circling round in the gloom; I could dimly see a solitary rider (later found to be Anthony Mildmay) vainly trying to make his horse jump the big open ditch further on. Otherwise, the race seemed to have passed out of view. Discontentedly I began to search for my whip.

I took some minutes to find it and had just begun my trudge back when my attention was attracted by a hail. There was my horse, held captive by a spectator whom I recognised as one of the lesser-known professional jockeys, and whom for the purposes of this narrative we will call H.C. Before I could thank him for saving me a long walk, he burst out: "Well, come on, don't you want to win?" I gaped at him. He continued, "Everyone else is down— jump on and finish the course and the race is yours!"

I suppose I should have rushed enthusiastically to my horse and bounded into the saddle, all agog. My true reactions were, I regret to say, far otherwise. No prospect has ever seemed more repugnant; I recoiled. I was cold and rather stiff. Almost five minutes had elapsed since I had fallen. It was absurd to think that not one of the sixteen runners had finished. How could anyone tell in this fog, anyhow? And yet . . . "Is my horse all right?" I asked weakly. "Absolutely," came the implacable reply. I fell silent, pondering on the dilemma with which I now saw I was confronted. On the one side was the prospect of a solo turn in cold blood over eleven Aintree fences, an ordeal which might well turn out to be quite pointless in the end, and which was made all the starker by the knowledge that my first fence would be Becher's Brook itself. On the other —well, suppose no one else *had* finished! What a fool one would feel, and look! I gazed frantically round. Anthony

Mildmay, still striving, was the only competitor visible. Silently, and quite unfairly, I cursed H.C.

A crowd of spectators had, meanwhile, gathered round and were showing signs of joining in the debate. In general, they supported H.C.; their manner was strongly reminiscent of a boxing crowd which, from the safe recesses of a hall, urges the smaller man to "go in and fight". I could delay my decision no longer—I gave in. Assuming an entirely bogus nonchalance, I mounted, turned my horse round and urged it rather forlornly in the general direction of Becher's Brook.

It says a great deal for September Air's courage that he judged it without demur. As we rose in the air, however, I saw that below me, on the landing side, was a crowd of spectators gazing with morbid satisfaction at the corpse of a horse stretched out upon the ground. I swooped upon them with a loud yell; they shrieked hideously in reply but scattered with such resolution that all survived my descent. Pursued by faint cries of indignation and dismay, I sped onwards, my courage rising. Over the Canal turn we sailed, and on over Valentine's and the big open ditch—over, in fact, Anthony Mildmay's horse, which had by this time descended into it. On we went; spectators, who by this time were walking about examining the fences, gaped to see this wild and muddy apparition careering round the course in what, as far as they knew, was the interval between races.

We turned into the straight, jumped the last two fences and passed the winning-post. The stands were almost deserted, but here and there knots of spectators turned to look, and some raised a rather stupefied cheer. H.C., beside himself with excitement, met me and led me in triumph to the winner's enclosure, into which we penetrated without opposition, its normal guardians having gone to watch the preliminaries to the next race. Soon, however, they realised that something unusual was occurring and sped back to their posts, scandalised, and bearing with them disillusion.

Apparently the enclosure had been occupied some ten minutes previously by the real winner; Tim Molony, then at the start of his career, had done much the same as I had, but rather earlier. He had fallen at the last fence, had scrambled on again and finished alone. Nobody could deny, however, that I was second, and I moved down to the humbler berth.

H.C. then vanished in search of the Press, to make sure, he said, that his part in the affair received due recognition. Meanwhile, I looked in vain for my connections—my wife, my trainer, the "lads", all usually immediately available to take my horse and submit their criticisms of my performance. Where were they? I was indignant. Eventually news of them arrived; after gazing for several anxious minutes into the fog, they had decided that I was not going to reappear; and bearing brandy, rugs, hot water-bottles and humane killers, they had quitted the stands and had sallied vaguely but valiantly forth into the gloom.

At last they returned. Amid a flood of explanations one fact, however, stood out pleasantly clear; I had won a stake of £200. We accordingly repaired to the bar to drink wine.

Next day I was back on duty at the military establishment in southern England in which I had found a niche after the disappearance of the 23rd Hussars. Here were the high armoured and technical experts, upon whose breakfast tables *Sporting Life* found no place. Here, surely, a merciful oblivion would reign. I was wrong. As I entered the ante-room of the Mess, I became aware that I was the object of very general interest. Then, to my horror, I discovered what H.C. had done; the sporting column of almost every paper recounted with relish and with some detail my antics of the day before, as seen through H.C.'s eyes.

Attracted by the buzz of conversation, the high officers rose and bent their sober gaze upon the headlines. The *Daily Mail*, I remember, had JOCKEY, TEN MINUTES LATE, THOUGHT HE'D WON. As the great ones read, their expressions became puzzled and noncommittal—was this affair creditable or discreditable; could it be classified as a good show or a bad show? It was a difficult question; there must be no hasty or ill-considered judgment. Said one: "This account reads, 'I persuaded the rider to remount'." Their expressions darkened: had there perhaps been a want of courage? The verdict hung in the balance; all was in suspense. At last, however, the clouds rolled back; the sun shone; I was acquitted. "Good show!" they said, "Good show!" and, shaking their heads, they went back to their offices, to their blueprints and their diagrams. All *so* much easier to understand.

CHAPTER SIX

Grand National

By the end of my first season I was fully launched on my all too brief steeplechasing career. September Air had won me a couple of small races, and one or two other owners had mounted me to their reasonable satisfaction. I was by now a steeplechasing addict, surrounded by Chase-forms, Racing Calendars, and copies of *Sporting Life*; spending all my time away from military duties on race-courses or in riding gallops in the hope of getting a chance mount.

The senior officers for whom I now worked were, as already indicated, uninterested in racing, and they regarded my frequent pleas for absence with a sort of weary indulgence. "Where's Blacker today?" one of them would ask, and usually he would get back a vague, "Oh, off on some horse thing he's doing." But provided I got through my not very exacting duties before leaving for the races, nobody worried much.

Steeplechasing was my first sporting love, and there is little doubt that it will probably be my last—in the comparatively inactive rôles of owner or amateur trainer. It is a sad thought that now I have joined the ranks of the comfortable, overcoated ex-amateur riders, I no longer frequent that select club, the race-course changing-room.

Across the unsaddling enclosure you would go and enter the weighing-room, to which the Stewards and officials have given a faintly intimidating air. On through this ante-chamber to the cosier atmosphere of the changing-room, with its benches round the walls and its centre filled up with tables covered in saddles, weight-cloths, bits of lead, crash helmets, whips and every imaginable bit of racing gear. Amiable confusion would be reigning there, presided over by elderly or middle-aged jockeys' valets dispensing kit and badinage with their clients who are dressing or seated round the walls. There is a warm aroma, composed of sweat, liniment, saddle-soap and cigarette smoke.

Steeplechase jockeys are the most friendly, cheerful, "rough with the smooth" people. They have far fewer pretensions than their counterparts on the flat—not surprisingly, for there is no room for pretension in a sport in which pride quite literally goes before a fall; in which the financial rewards are far from great, and in which the saying "horses can make fools of us all" is nowhere more true. The most celebrated National Hunt rider will spare a word of encouragement and congratulation for the most insignificant of youngsters and the greenest of amateurs.

The dressing-room is full of cheerful backchat and leg-pulling, dying down to a mutter as the room empties for the next race and building up again to a crescendo as the mudstained crowd pours back through the door, commenting in lurid and uninhibited terms on the events of the past few minutes. Then, as the last race is run and the dusk and fog begin to close in, the groups of tough, weary men, over-coated now, file cheerfully out to a chorus of "Goodnight, Jim", "G'night, Tom, see you at Doncaster!" "Yes—if it doesn't freeze—g'night . . ." And another meeting is over. They pass all too quickly, these winter meetings, inter-rupted as they are by fog, floods, frost and snow. Soon the National Hunt Meeting at Cheltenham, and the Grand National, are upon us; then we are talking about our plans for the next season.

My second season began depressingly. In racing, as in roulette, luck seems to go in runs. If Fortune decides to frown upon you she will do so consistently, and for a definite, sometimes prolonged period. Your mounts will all run unaccountably badly, and some will go lame. Others will contrive to fall, and if they can kick you at the same time so much, apparently, the better. If you are riding a horse which prefers firm going, the course on which you are due to ride is bound to be deluged with rain. Perhaps on a course in another part of England it will remain dry, but there you are sure to be riding a horse which likes the ground soft. Races from which your horse has been withdrawn subsequently prove to be the very contests which it would certainly have won, and just as a suitable race is due the meeting is at once abandoned through frost. All this is very demoralising, and on such occasions it is best to remember that all bad things come to an end one day.

Then Fortune, apparently overcome with remorse, will turn to you with a charming smile, and all will at once go right. Where before you lost races by a short head and were condemned as a jockey seriously lacking in judgment and nerve, now, using precisely the same tactics, you will win them by the same margin and be hailed as a promising, skilled and resolute rider. The frowns of owners and trainers will turn to smiles, and in the various race-course bars you will be treated to champagne instead of lager beer. All this at the whim of Fortune.

In the autumn of 1947 I underwent one of these black periods. This was all the worse because I was due to return to my regiment in Germany in the New Year and time was therefore getting short. Before I departed I was determined to establish my reputation, so that whenever I returned to England I should be sure of a few good rides; and I also had a very strong desire to feature in the 1948 Grand National. Neither ambition got off to a good start.

By the end of December, and within a week before my return to Germany, I had to acknowledge that I was having an extremely unsuccessful season. I had ridden hardly any winners, and few owners or trainers seemed noticeably anxious to employ me. My Grand National plans were in ruins. These had centred round September Air, now qualified for the race through his rather fortunate second in the previous year's Stanley Chase. Although it was clear by now that he was not a really good horse, he would not, from the point of view of class, have been disgraced in the big race. We felt, however, that it would be as well to let him have a further experience of the Aintree fences before deciding definitely. Thus we had competed in the Valentine Chase at the 1947 November meeting. Our precautions had been fully justified, as was soon made clear. At Becher's Brook I took a fall which I shall not easily forget. I have a vivid memory of horse and rider completely upside down in the air and of myself thinking that this must certainly be the most spectacular fall ever to occur, even at Liverpool. I woke in the first-aid room behind the stands, a room which I seem to have visited with distressing frequency during my brief racing career, and found that I was being given—rather surprisingly—strong whisky. On my recovery, which was speedy, I reluctantly decided that to attempt a Grand National on September Air would on the whole be unwise. This decision was most firmly endorsed by my wife, whose two trips to Aintree since her marriage had each been altogether too exciting for her comfort. Indeed, long before my second venture there she had castigated my plans for riding September Air in the National as being completely mad. For by no means the first or last time I had in the end to agree that she was right. Nevertheless this was all very disappointing, and the last days of 1947 saw me packing my clothes for Germany in a disillusioned mood.

But now my trainer, Alec Kilpatrick, to whose kindness, skill and faith in me I attribute what little success I ever achieved, parted company with his stable jockey. He rang me up and asked me to ride Sir John at Manchester on January 4th. This was certainly one of the biggest honours I have ever been accorded, for the horse was the best in the stable, had been extremely expensive to buy, and gave promise of much brilliance. So far, however, in the few races he had run, luck had not come his way, and since coming over from Ireland he had yet to win. His elderly owner, whose first horse this was and whose expectation of success bore little relation to the realities of racing, was becoming restive. With his eyes fixed upon the Grand National, he was disturbed at the non-success of his expensive purchase in smaller races. Now there was no stable jockey. After much discussion Alec and he decided to take a chance with the stable amateur, out of luck and inexperienced as he was.

Here, I at once realised, was the big chance which the struggling understudy eventually gets in Hollywood films. Fail, and my racing ambitions were temporarily at an end. Succeed, and a ride in the Grand National was almost certain. Further, if the stable continued without a regular jockey many other opportunities would be sure to offer themselves, for in such circumstances I was fully prepared to fly back from Germany from time to time whenever I could get away. Having wired to my regiment to say I would be two days late, I joyfully accepted.

I had never been on a horse like Sir John before. He gave you the sort of Bentley-like feel which only really good horses do. He suffered throughout his short life from being asked to do too much too soon; if he had been able to progress unhurriedly from stage to stage there is no knowing where he might have gone. He was killed two seasons later, having won several good races but without having fulfilled the promise which I am certain he possessed. He gave me a magnificent ride at Manchester; in the best musical comedy tradition, the understudy took his chance. We won convincingly from a good field.

Afterwards, the race-course bar was full of sweetness and light; everyone congratulated everyone else and my engagement to ride Sir John in the National was announced to the Press. My chief fear was that the excitement might prove too much for the owner, who had a weak heart, but I afterwards found that so long as we were successful there was nothing to be afraid of. A defeat, however, often had the gravest results upon his health, and on one occasion the only glimpse I had of him after the race was his palpitating form being hastily led away by his doctor. I believe it was only the thought of his horse running in the Grand National which kept him alive at all.

I departed to Germany in a great state of jubilation, which the broadside I later received from the War Office for arriving two days late did nothing to impair. In any event there was extremely little to do then in Germany, and practically no soldiers to do it with. I spent some of the time after my return in planning the best way of playing the part of the Kilpatrick stable jockey while situated several hundred miles away across the North Sea. North Germany was very inaccessible at that time and the nearest functioning airport was Amsterdam. Every time I was offered a ride in England I would jump on the leave train bound for the Hook of Holland and disembark unobtrusively from it at Utrecht. This was illegal, but I always disappeared down a subway before the infuriated shouts of military policemen could be translated into action. Half an hour away by train was Amsterdam and its airport. By leaving my barracks in Germany in mid-morning I could be in London for dinner and at the race-course in plenty of time next day—slow going by modern standards but the best I could devise under the circumstances. My return was engineered by the reverse process; the only tricky part here was getting on the leave train at Utrecht. In this way I kept my absences as brief as possible, though the frequency of these trips depended greatly on how generous owners were in helping out with travelling expenses.

I cannot pretend that this was a satisfactory or a cheap way of keeping my race-riding going, but I was determined that at all costs I would hang on to my engagement for Sir

John, and indeed to as many of my other rides as possible. By now I knew all too well how fickle and forgetful owners are apt to become. Only allow Sir John to be ridden once by a professional because I could not get home to partner him, and together they would be bound to win some smart and expensive race. I had no illusions at all about the likelihood of a change of rider then being gaily announced to the Press without a thought for what I felt about it. No discomfort or inconvenience was too great to prevent such an intolerable possibility.

It was just as well that there was not much soldiering to be done in Germany during the six weeks between the middle of February and the end of March. For most of this period I was commanding the regiment, for its Colonel, Alec Scott, had gone off to join the Olympic show-jumping team. I made a series of racing trips back to England, where I eventually achieved my aim of riding in the Grand National. I sat, and miraculously passed, the Staff College Examination, and I became a father. Two days after the Grand National I was removed suddenly to hospital to have my appendix out. It was a crowded period but, despite the appendix, on the whole a very happy and successful one, though I sometimes wished all the various events could have been rather further spaced out.

The racing trips to England were reasonably successful, and included a nice, unexpected double at the Grand Military Meeting. Sir John ran in two National Trials, was third in one and fell in the other. He was potentially a brilliant jumper but even round normal courses he was apt to make one serious error, and I already suspected that this failing would cost him dear round Aintree. He was in fact running in the big race at least one season sooner than he should have, but by then the die had been cast. His owner, poor old man, was becoming increasingly decrepit. He was determined to see his horse run at Liverpool this year, for he had more than a suspicion (entirely justified, as it turned out) that he was unlikely to see another. So we travelled to Aintree in Grand National week more hopeful than confident.

Before breakfast on the morning of the race, all the horses are out exercising on the Aintree course. This is an interesting, even a fascinating, occasion. In front of the enormous empty stands, with only a few isolated knots of people to watch, the entries for the great race and their riders move informally to and fro. There is easy chat between jockeys, and the atmosphere is light and jocular; the tension of the day has not yet begun to build up. Here on this occasion were Anthony Mildmay (looking very wasted and ill) on Cromwell, John Hislop on Cloncarrig, Bryan Marshall on Royland Roy. Lord Bicester's pair, Roimond and Silver Fame, with Dick Black and Martin Molony riding, cantered past together, as did Arthur Thompson on Sheila's Cottage and Ron Smyth on Klaxton. Sir John moved smoothly and well, apparently unmoved by the occasion. It was a crisp spring morning, giving promise of a lovely day, and we left the course for our hotel—and for the newspapers, with feelings of regret.

The sporting columns of the daily press were so full of the big race, and so hysterical about the enormous sums which had been wagered, that merely to read them produced a feeling of suspense. I very soon settled down to an Agatha Christie novel, but reality could not be wholly banished and nagged uncomfortably at the back of the mind. The morning plodded by, but at midday we were off to the course—an early start for fear of languishing too long in a traffic jam.

When we arrived at Aintree there were still two hours to go before the race. I had no need to walk the course and wandered about aimlessly, killing time. Occasionally I ran into a friend but conversation was apt to be distrait and fitful, and I seldom delayed him long. It was extremely difficult to take much interest in the earlier races, which were on the flat, but gradually I succeeded in getting through to the moment when it was time to change.

Forty-five jockeys changing simultaneously in two very small rooms are not conducive to a grim and serious atmosphere, and the tension lightened at once. The dressing-room was indeed a comfortable little island upon which all the inhabitants talked the same language and had a common understanding of the job in hand. The valets, too, understood and had just the right word for the occasion. I felt sorry when I was changed and had to sally forth again into the sea of curious faces and the mounting feeling of excitement. Before this, however, we had to weigh out. This was a prolonged affair, and while the queue of jockeys waited their turn the news-reel camera clicked and flash-lights exploded. There were then another forty-five long minutes before mounting and, being changed, I was at once a marked man. Acquaintances forced their way to my side and made jovial remarks. They had obviously lunched well, some had cigars, and all had warm overcoats and looks of great contentment. I felt deeply envious, and somewhat provoked when several of them accused me of looking very white about the gills. This, although I denied it, was perfectly true, in fact if anything I was green, but I like to think that this was caused more by my appendix, which had to be hastily and unexpectedly removed two days later, than by fright.

We were back in the dressing-room for the last time before the race, tying on caps and sorting out whips. Then during the last few minutes an odd, strained hush fell on the room. The pseudo-jocular remarks died away, and nobody seemed to be able to think of anything more to say. We just sat quietly with bent heads, playing with our whips. Then there was a shout of "Jockeys please!" and we all shuffled out.

There was an immense crowd round the paddock, and inside the space seemed to be full of owners, trainers and perambulating horses. A moment or two of rather strained conversation before we mounted, and, pursued by shouts of "Good luck!", we were led past the stands, now a blur of white faces packed together and towering up high above the course. Most horses, sensing the excitement in the air, became restive.

Past the stands, one by one the horses turned about, the grooms released their hold on the reins, and the field cantered down to the start. As my groom, an old friend, let go of the bridle with a pat on Sir John's neck and a quiet "Good luck, sir!" to me, I had the odd and rather lonely sensation that everything that a trainer and a groom could do had now been done. The rest was up to me and Sir John.

Forty-five horses at the start walked round for a moment, and then lined up, jostling for position. The flag was raised. The gate flew up, and in an irregular surge the field rolled forward towards the first fence.

The first fence of the National is over four hundred yards from the start. It has a sizeable drop and is the first of five similar fences leading to the worst drop of all, Becher's Brook. The size of the field, and the number of loose horses which soon materialise make every jockey determined to get a good start. Consequently the field, having gathered momentum over the intervening four hundred yards, arrive at the first fence travelling at considerable speed. The horses, all unsuspecting, then encounter the drop, which, if they are going too fast, is quite capable of throwing them forward and bringing them down even if they have not actually touched the fence. Hence the number of falls there often are at the first few fences.

My first sensation was one of surprise that the field got so strung out on the way to the first fence. I was about half way back and there was no feeling of being jostled at all. I knew the first fence of old and, determined not to be caught out by it, steadied Sir John as much as I could. Impressed by the size of the fence, he rose high above it and plummeted innocently down into the drop. He touched ground with a gasp of dismay about a foot lower than he expected, fell on his nose and got up again, much wiser. All round were cracks, thuds, rendings, flying earth and horses' legs waving in the air. On the ground, muddied figures bunched tensely till the storm had passed.

Over the next three fences the same scenes were repeated in gradually diminishing intensity, and as the field grew smaller the loose horses began to appear. Some of these cantered sensibly off into the middle of the course, well out of the way, but the majority galloped sheep-like over the fences, accompanying the race. Loose horses are quite unpredictable; one which has jumped two fences soberly and well may suddenly elect to go through the wing of the next, taking you with it. Another may stop broadside across the fence or may cannon violently into you as you jump. At the fence before Becher's I was baulked by a loose horse and for a moment was in trouble, but somehow survived. Becher's loomed up and Sir John, meeting it in his stride, jumped it brilliantly. This is, I believe, the most thrilling sensation which riding, in any form, can offer. To sail through the air at that speed and from that height, with your horse perfectly balanced, and to be confident that all will be well when you land, is a joy which one does not forget.

A great many horses fall at the fence following Becher's and I have heard jockeys say they dislike it more than any other on the course. This is odd, because it appears to be one of the easiest, being a plain fence with no drop. It may be that by this time the horses are expecting a drop and fumble their landing, or it may be that Becher's has shaken their nerve. At all events, it is the only fence on the course that has since been lowered. I have never had trouble with it, nor did I on this occasion, and we galloped with growing confidence on towards the Canal Turn. This left-handed turn is extremely sharp, and, in the National, as you rise at the fence you seem to be jumping straight towards a solid phalanx of people not many yards away. It is essential to jump slightly crossways, or it becomes very difficult to negotiate the turn. As we landed over Valentine's I tried to take stock of the situation. There were about twenty of us left, galloping in a fairly compact bunch down the line of fences leading towards the stands and the end of the first circuit. I was about in the centre, and I could see that John Hislop on Cloncarrig was in the lead. But just as I had identified him his heels and his horse's tail flew up in the air and they disappeared from view, and from the race.

We cleared the Anchor Bridge fence, rejoined the race-course and galloped along the long stretch of open leading to the stands. At this point there is first a plain fence, then the Chair—the big open ditch. As we rode into this plain fence I could feel that we were absolutely out of stride and were bound to hit it. A moment of agonized effort, then *Crash!*—a splintering and crackling of wood, a frantic un-successful effort by Sir John to regain his feet and a thud as we hit the ground. We were out of it.

I walked back to watch the finish, in company with another jockey who had fallen at the same fence. Soon the leaders were in view again as they came on to the race-course for the second time. There appeared to be only four in it. First of the Dandies was leading from two mares, Zahia and Sheila's Cottage, while Cromwell, ridden by Anthony Mildmay, was following a few lengths behind.

Anthony Mildmay had been the victim of a celebrated hard-luck story in the second Grand National to be won by Reynoldstown, before the war. On his own horse Davy Jones he had jumped the penultimate fence well clear of Reynoldstown, whose jockey, Fulke Walwyn, had almost given up hope of victory. The story of what happened then is a well-known racing nightmare; the buckle of Davy Jones's reins came undone and, reinless, his rider could not prevent him from running out at the last fence. Now, in 1948, Fate probably repeated the trick, though in a less obvious way.

Three fences from home Anthony's backbone, as a result of a racing injury some time earlier, seized up in a position which locked him helpless and rigid, head and shoulders bowed, in one position. Temporarily almost paralysed, and quite unable to help Cromwell, or indeed do anything but sit there, he was carried past the winning-post third. The horse seemed to me to have had plenty of running left in him, and it was cruel that this great sportsman should have been yet again denied a fair chance at the ambition for which he tried so hard and which he never achieved.

This tragedy was not so obvious to me, as I stood at the last fence watching, as the drama of Zahia. This mare was level with Sheila's Cottage and First of the Dandies at the last fence but one, and going every bit as well. Suddenly she left the course. Either she had run out, or much more likely, her jockey had mistaken the way which, in those days, before the course was clearly marked off, was quite a possible thing to do at that point. The dismounted jockeys standing near the fence waved and shouted frantically to warn her rider, but in that momentary disastrous error a great chance of winning the National had gone, never to recur.

First of the Dandies and Sheila's Cottage approached the last fence together, accompanied by the roar of the crowd, a frenzied tumultuous wave of sound. In the straight the mare drew clear, and the two horses passed the post with about a length between them. Behind them came Anthony Mildmay on Cromwell, and at long intervals about five more survivors straggled in. Meanwhile the victor had disappeared into the throng, through which we eventually forced ourselves. In the unsaddling enclosure, surrounded by dense masses of cheering people, stood Arthur Thompson, the winning jockey and the hero of the hour. At the same time, unnoticed by the crowd, I saw a small, utterly miserable figure slipping unobtrusively back into the dressing-room—the rider of Zahia. As I followed him in I reflected, not for the first time, that racing was a chancy game.

CHAPTER SEVEN

Modern Pentathlon

At the end of 1948 I found myself back in England, beginning a year's course at the Camberley Staff College. Racing ambitions had, for the time being to be modified. My fellow students were on the whole a very pleasant lot, and many became my friends, but the atmosphere of the course, beneath all the *bonhomie* and military humour, was serious and even competitive. Although our task for the year was to study the conduct of war and to learn how to be Staff Officers, we all realised that its most relevant and immediate effect on us would be to grade us for future employment.

This aspect of the course was naturally much played down by the staff. Embarrassed looks would pass over our instructors' faces if any student was tactless enough to imply that we realised its existence, and thus spoil the illusion that we were one big, happy family selflessly studying the technique of our profession. It was, of course, obvious that the students who did best would get the more interesting and worthwhile appointments at the end of the year; at the same time we vied with each other in thinking up unattractive and lowly posts with which to torment ourselves in our moments of depression.

There never was a year, in my experience, in which it was more important to get the priorities right. For I was resolved that there should be priorities. While Staff College work was without doubt the highest, I was not going to pass the year as a kind of military monk. I saw no reason, for example, to give up any more of my steeplechasing mounts than I had to. It was still possible to improvise ways of getting to the races and, from this point of view at least, Camberley could hardly have been better located.

It was inevitably a losing battle. Owners and trainers are not going to be satisfied for very long with a jockey who can usually only appear on Saturdays, and, heart-breakingly, all my best rides slipped out of my grasp and were allotted to other more favourably placed riders. A few, however, remained. One of these horses was due to run at Kempton Park on a Tuesday afternoon in February —a working day during the early, intense part of the course.

I looked at the programme. On Tuesday we were due to write our first operation order, starting at ten-thirty in the morning and handing our efforts in before five. It would be an important exercise, our first significant bit of written work, and one to be taken very seriously. We could, however, write it unsupervised, though we would not receive the question paper until ten-thirty. The race at Kempton was at two-thirty. I would have to be at the course by a quarter-to-two at the very latest. That meant leaving Camberley before one o'clock. Somehow I would have to write an operation order, for which (allowing for lunch) five and a half hours had been allotted, in just under two and a half. If I could not get it done in time I should at best become gravely unpopular with the authorities and, at worst, the consequences could be disastrous. On the other hand if I accepted the ride I must at all costs get to Kempton by a quarter-to-two; it was unthinkable to allow a trainer to send a horse miles to a meeting, inform the owner and then be let down by the non-arrival of the jockey. I accepted the ride.

We were always being told at the Staff College to

exercise foresight and to plan ahead, and I now took the advice to heart. On the day before my race the Staff College was studying and discussing a tactical situation culminating in an attack. All sorts of solutions and plans were propounded by students for this attack, and at the end of the day we were given the school solution. As I read it my heart leapt. Nothing could be more obvious than that the school solution for this attack would form the basis of the operation order which we were due to write next day. There were a great many details, particularly those of timing, which I would not know until I received the question paper in the morning, but I could certainly break the back of the exercise forthwith.

Into the night I laboured with this premature birth. I sat down at ten-thirty next morning knowing that all hung on my guess being right. When the white slips of paper containing the requirement were handed round I was conscious of great relief; it was as I had forecast and I should now be able to reach Kempton easily. Shortly after midday, to the astonishment of the remainder of my syndicate, I rose self-consciously to my feet with the completed exercise and left the room to drop it into my instructor's box.

I had a splendid ride at Kempton and all the cobwebs of the classroom were blown out of me. In a good finish the horse was third, about the position which both owner and trainer expected it to occupy and so they were satisfied. It is wonderful how quickly you forget your worries if you move temporarily into a different world, particularly one which cares nothing for operation orders. I drove home refreshed and exhilarated.

At the Staff College the students were meanwhile fighting their way through the exercise, and the staff were able to relax round the television set. Suddenly, and much to his surprise, my instructor found himself watching one of his students, whom he had left sitting with furrowed brow over an operation order, riding a finish at Kempton Park.

This caused a stir, and after some discussion he went to my syndicate room to see if perhaps I had a double. Having drawn blank there, he went to his box and found my completed exercise reposing inside.

I was not, of course, out of the wood until he had corrected it and discovered whether it would pass muster. For some reason, presumably owing to my very clear realisation that this of all exercises had got to be good, it found considerable favour. Indeed, the general view was that anyone who could write an operation order like that in two hours must be a budding Napoleon, for I saw no reason to say anything about my midnight oil. Although I was not able to maintain this spurious reputation for the rest of the year, my trip to Kempton fell inadvertently but undoubtedly into the category of military one-upmanship.

On the whole, however, I found that it was not possible to ride seriously during the course—and that is the only way to ride if you expect trainers to put you up in valuable races and on good horses. I had to look for another horizon for which to aim.

One evening I was having a drink with Percy Legard in London. Percy is a most versatile and enterprising athlete, and while serving in my regiment before the war he had been a member of the British Pentathlon Team at the Los Angeles Olympic Games. "Why don't you take up the Modern Pentathlon?" he said. "You can ride, you can run, and you'll soon learn the other three things." This was such a new idea to me that I dismissed it out of hand, but later it came back to me and I began to toy with it. I really knew nothing at all about the sport and after a while I took steps to put this right.

To quote from the official history of the competition: "The athlete is required to ride a horse across country, fence with an epée, shoot with a pistol . . . with the greatest precision, swim 330 yards and conclude by running two and a half miles across country—all this in the space of five days." Each competitor receives a certain number of points according to the standard of his performance in each event, and victory goes to the man with the highest total. Thus the competitor skilful enough to score the permitted maximum in every event cannot be beaten—but he would have to be a very remarkable all-rounder.

The Modern Pentathlon is a sport for the all-rounder, for the man who wants to excel but not to specialise, who has no urge—or more likely has not the ability—to become, for example, a tennis champion or an international runner. It is a good competition for those whose motto is "try anything once", for there can be very few people alive who do not have to learn at least one or two of the five events from scratch.

When I eventually decided to try the Modern Pentathlon, I did so with much misgiving about my ability to achieve a competitive standard in all five events. I had ridden all my life and was a good runner, but there it ended. I could swim, but in a curious shrimp-like movement which demanded enormous expenditure of energy to achieve any noticeable forward motion. I had never taken part in a pistol-shooting contest and was fairly certain what the results would have been if I had; I had never touched an epée in my life. But I soon found that this is one of the joys of the competition, which seems specially designed to prevent one man sweeping the board. When practising with others it is not necessary to be despondent when you see a fellow-competitor cleaving the waters of the swimming-bath with the precision of an otter. Perhaps you will shortly see him on a horse, an apprehensive, sweaty figure with those legs which had just looked so effective in the water, oscillating weakly to and fro in a vain effort to get his mount to jump. Conversely, when you have just demolished your opponents in a cross-country run, it is extremely good for your soul if one of the vanquished then prods you into subjection at the point of his epée. In general, I found that if one persevered, and retained a sense of proportion, it was possible to reach a stage where one would not necessarily be outclassed in the competition as a whole.

The riding event usually takes place over a cross-country course of some two and a half miles, and I soon found that there were two important requirements for success. The first was that since the jumps were solid the only faults you could incur were from a refusal—or a fall; consequently the deciding factor between a number of clear rounds was time. Thus you could throw elegance to the winds and concentrate on speed. Secondly, you could not ride your own horse, but had to draw your mount by lot from a pool of animals provided, for the British Championship at any rate, by various military units. These animals, in the course of their experience, had nearly all learnt the important lesson that it was far less uncomfortable to refuse to leave the ground than to leave it with inexperienced riders on their backs. Thus you had to be prepared to do a considerable amount of urging if you were to avoid a refusal.

The swimming event was a terrible trial to me. After I had timed myself over the full distance of 330 yards I had to face the fact that to stand any chance at all I would have to learn an effective stroke, and stop imitating a shrimp. Here I was lucky in that the Aldershot indoor bath was reasonably close to the Staff College, and so every lunch period would find me there, a solitary figure ploughing up and down in blue, chlorinated water. Mr Dixon, the attendant, was kind enough to tell me roughly how to achieve a crawl, and every now and then would turn his head from hanging up towels or stoking the boiler in order to shout advice or rebukes at me. No professional instructor was going to spend his lunch interval at the baths, and so perforce by this somewhat rudimentary system I slowly learnt. I would flash back on my motor-bicycle to the Staff College in time for a very quick lunch and a resumption of work—which I probably performed all the better for having taken a good deal of exercise.

I never became a good swimmer although I eventually learnt the crawl. I doubt if it is possible to become expert if you are past thirty before you start to acquire the technique, and in any case Mr Dixon told me with truth that I lacked the physical quality of buoyancy. This meant that if I stopped swimming I sank. Somebody who is naturally buoyant floats. This is most unfair; half my energy had to be directed towards keeping afloat, while my more buoyant opponents saved all their energies for moving forwards. I found my swimming contests exhausting and frustrating; very often the faster I seemed to be swimming the slower I found I had gone; in any event, I always swallowed quantities of very nasty water. Still, through taking part in the Pentathlon I have at least learnt to swim a great deal better than I could before.

I learnt fencing by invading a gymnasium at Aldershot and dragooning one of the physical training sergeants into teaching me. It was hot and restricting in the white padded clothing and I never became a fencing enthusiast. I could see that it might become fascinating to the dedicated, but for me it was all too complicated and rule-bound. I fear I lack patience in the acquiring of skill in these very exact sports. (For this same, and deplorable, reason I have never been able in the riding world to get excited about dressage, which in its ceremony and its Continental terminology reminds me very much of fencing.) However, in a somewhat rudimentary fashion I became a tolerable epée swordsman. Pistol-shooting was rather easier to learn, though it is just as difficult a sport in which to become an expert. Both fencing and pistol-shooting are, however, sports in which application, a quick eye, and a reasonably steady nerve will carry you through however great the initial ignorance. Thus I became a "pentathlete".

Practising for the Pentathlon provided an excellent distraction from Staff College work, and by good fortune fitted in well with my next appointment. This was to the Ministry of Defence in London, as a member of the Joint

Planning Staff. I became immersed in secret planning studies for military operations, and worked long hours which made racing as difficult as it had been at Camberley. It was however possible to practise for the Pentathlon, and indeed it was a relief to be able to fling down my pencil on, for example, a treatise on the strategic importance of Cocos Island, and dive into the swimming-bath at the RAC. I would shoot my pistol and run round the running-track at the Duke of York's Barracks in Chelsea. I joined the London Fencing Club, where Professor Delzi did his best, but in vain, to inspire me with some of his own panache. By now I had found that success in the Pentathlon depended, as it does in so many ventures, very largely on the amount of trouble you were prepared to take.

Training for the Pentathlon may be strenuous but it is never dull, and you never get a chance to feel complacent about your progress. One morning in the swimming-bath you may triumphantly master the crawl, only to develop an uncontrollable twitch in your pistol hand in the evening. The indifferent rider may be rendered so stiff that his fencing reactions, or his running, are affected. You are seldom quite sure whether hope or despair is uppermost. This uncertainty is one of the competition's greatest assets; preparation for it is a strict exercise in perseverance, patience and good humour. Perhaps that is why the competitors are usually so pleasant to meet, and why the atmosphere of the meetings both at home and overseas is invariably so friendly and sporting.

I was beginning to achieve some success in the British Championships—so called although precious few civilians ever joined in at that time. Our regimental team of three won the regimental championship for three consecutive years, and I slowly rose up the individual ranking list until I was amongst at least the first six. This, by world standards, did not mean much, for although the Pentathlon features in the Olympic Games and is a major sport in several countries, particularly in Scandinavia, it has never

Receiving the 1954 Grand Military
Gold Cup from the Queen Mother.

A mercifully uncritical audience.

At the Brighton Show, 1958. Left to right: *Jack Talbot-Ponsonby, D. Bunn, Pat Smythe and the Author.*

Jumping on Stromboli in floodlight, Chile 1959.

really caught on in this country and draws its recruits from too restricted a circle. The most strenuous efforts have recently been made to publicise the Modern Pentathlon, and it is very difficult to see that more could have been done to put it on the sporting map. These efforts have not really succeeded, and my personal feeling is that, particularly in the television age, the British sporting public likes a spectacle, and the Pentathlon does not provide this. In none of the individual events is the standard of the competitors anything very spectacular. The fact that it is a triumph of versatility and training to have achieved the standards they have, not in one event but in five, is not appreciated because it does not catch the eye; the sport has little spectator-value because the spectators are not discerning—or will not take the trouble to be. I thought this was the natural order of things everywhere until I took part in the 1951 World Championships in Sweden as a member of the British team.

In Sweden the Modern Pentathlon really means something, and the World Championships are regarded with much the same degree of interest as the Badminton Three Day Event in Great Britain. Large crowds attended each of the five events, which were fully reported and illustrated in the Press, and the general public were obviously fully conversant with the finer points of the competition. Autograph hunters were operating on much the same scale as they do at the White City International Horse Show, and the excitement generated in the closing stages was an eye-opener to the British competitors.

Our team consisted of Jack Lumsdaine, a Flight-Lieutenant in the RAF, Jervis Percy, a subaltern in the Durham Light Infantry, and myself. Marine Jock Wood completed this suitably inter-service team as reserve, and the imperturbable and cheerful Colonel Errol Lonsdale was team captain. We touched down at Hälsingborg on a clear October day. There was a fresh autumnal bite in the air, and the blue and green uniforms of our hosts stood

D

out gaily against a background of russet trees. After a friendly welcome we were politely separated from our wives, who were whisked away from the scene of operations and installed well out of sight and contact some miles off. On our arrival at the camp at which we were to live we got our first taste of the somewhat febrile atmosphere which competitors produce when they live at close quarters with their rivals. As we entered the gates a gasping crowd of track-suited Brazilians swept past us, their coach mouthing incomprehensibly at a stop-watch. Across the passage of our hut lay an American, doing press-ups, whilst through an open door a perspiring Dane could be observed having a massage. Some Finns, swimsuits in hand, saluted us solemnly on their way to the baths. We feverishly changed into our track-suits, wondering which event we had better practise first.

For the three days preceding the competition we practised frantically. This was really rather absurd as we had already practised hard for several months now, and it was far too late to make much difference. However, everyone else did, and we caught the infection. There was great competition for the shooting-range and the swimming-bath. To get a clear run at the range you had to be up at about six-thirty, and as the swimming-bath was thirty miles away and was not available till nine o'clock at night we did not get to bed much before midnight. In between we sped from one practice ground to the next and even if there was an occasional hour for slumber in the afternoons one was invariably disturbed by anxious clickings of pistols and experimental clashings of sword blades. It was, quite unnecessarily, a restless period.

We did, however, have time to appraise our opponents' probable form. The Swedes and Finns, grim of face, were highly competent in all departments, the Danes cheerful and highly incompetent. The Americans looked as if they would be good when they had more practice, the Swiss pretty good and the French only fair. The Italians did not look up to much, while the Brazilians were clearly built for swimming rather than running.

It was a relief when the competition began. The riding event came first, and was on the whole enjoyable. The Swedes had laid out quite a formidable but entirely fair cross-country course of some three miles, and had provided first-class horses for us to ride. All these horses were of approximately equal standard and very well schooled; the only difficulty we experienced was that they did not always respond to British aids and thus took a little getting used to. One of the Swedes showed us how to make a curious smacking sound with the lips at which all Swedish horses are trained to accelerate. We tried it, and the effect on our mounts was indeed electrifying.

I ought undoubtedly to have won the riding event, and only lost it through trying to be too clever. In order to cut a corner I advanced on one fence at a trot, hoping to be able to turn as I landed. What I did not then realise was that Swedish Army horses are not trained to such fancy tricks; they jump at a gallop or not at all. My animal stopped. I smacked my lips furiously. It plunged violently forward and got itself astride the obstacle where it see-sawed for much too long. Furious with myself, I hurled it round the rest of the course at top speed, but could only muster eighth place out of twenty-seven.

We had high hopes of Jervis Percy, however, who appeared to have done a clear round. The multitude assembled in a field to hear the results; a dais had been erected in the middle and the first three competitors were to mount this, under their respective national flags and to the strains of their respective national anthems. As we were waiting the blow fell. Jervis was accused (falsely as it turned out) of having had a refusal. Otherwise he would have been third. We demanded that the results should be re-checked, but while this was happening, two Swedes occupied the first two places on the dais and a Finn usurped the third. Flags were broken and Scandinavian anthems filled the air. Just as the ceremony ended we heard that Jervis really was third. We would dearly have liked to have made them perform this little ceremony again, in order that the Union Jack (and Jervis) should have been suitably displayed. No British competitor had featured in this ceremony since the war, and it was irritating to be done out of it now. However, we consoled ourselves with the fact that we had made a reasonable start and so far, out of the nine teams competing, we were third.

The fencing next day was in two sessions, one in the morning and the other at seven o'clock in the evening, so that the populace could attend. There is no doubt that you need to go abroad to see fencing at its best; a match between two stolid and undemonstrative Englishmen entirely misses the true spirit of the sport. But observe an Italian in combat with a Swede, a Frenchman in mortal grapple with a Brazilian! See the *élan* with which they dart and posture, hear the exultant yell with which they penetrate their opponent's guard. What panache! What fun!

We English plodded steadily through the day and were not displeased to end up with Jack eighth and myself twelfth, with Jervis rather lower. Elsewhere passions ran high and some of the other teams were temporarily not on speaking terms. We tried to steer clear of the prevailing acrimony, but in the end we fell foul of the Italians. The dispute, which became highly technical, revolved round somebody's foot, which was either in or out of bounds when he had administered the *coup-de-grâce*. In the end we gained the judge's decision but lost the friendship of the Italians, one of whom refused to shake hands with us and remained in the highest possible dudgeon for the rest of the meeting.

The next day, the pistol-shooting, was a strain. The range was two hundred yards from our huts, and we lay on our beds waiting our turn. Marine Wood was to summon us one by one. He was getting rather bored with being reserve and was, moreover, a far better shot himself than any of us; this was, therefore, a doubly trying day for him. He normally spent part of his time imitating the foreigners, whose antics convulsed him with merriment, and the rest in making pungent Glaswegian comments on events in general. I usually much appreciated his rather basic form of humour, but feared that our performances at the butts were all too likely to be his target for today.

Pistol-shooting is an uncomfortable business. In the Pentathlon you have to fire twenty rounds snap at a figure target. To do any good at all in international class you must get all twenty on, and fairly centrally too. One shot off (and nothing is easier) puts you right down the list. "Two off" is a disaster.

Jervis went first, and soon we could hear distant crackles of fire as the early competitors took their places in the arena. After an interval Jack went. Later Wood put his head round the door for me. "Paircy put two off," he announced with glum relish.

We walked gloomily down to the pistol-range. A large throng of spectators surrounded the arena in which stood the six competitors then performing. The twenty rounds were fired off in four details of five shots each; after each detail there was a prolonged pause while the judges went down the line of targets marking the hits. A good "group" of shots would bring a ripple of applause, a bad one a sympathetic silence, while the non-playing captain of the unfortunate competitor would feverishly search the target for any holes which the judges might conceivably have missed. While this was going on the firers stood round with a strained nonchalance, making insincere conversation.

A group of the other competitors was standing at the back of the arena, looking at the targets of those who had already fired. Jervis was not among them—clearly he wished to be alone and I hoped someone had taken the pistol from him. We gazed at the "used" targets; some, particularly those of the Brazilians, Americans and Swedes, showed quite remarkably good scores; the highest was 195 out of a possible 200, and others were very close. The bad ones, I was relieved to see, were, however, very bad; they elicited from Wood some colourful remarks which cannot be quoted in detail.

Jack was just finishing—he got twenty on and had shot very steadily for a score of 178. He would be about twelfth, we reckoned. His heat had been badly delayed by a Finn whose ammunition consistently misfired. "It is Russian," he explained. Eventually, a kindly American came to the rescue with some ammunition made in Detroit, after which there was no more trouble. Soon my heat was called.

There is no doubt that competitive pistol-shooting before a large audience is an ordeal which only experience can diminish. On most big occasions in other sports it is not difficult to appear outwardly calm, but then you are not required to hold a pistol at arm's length with a rock-steady hand. This was my first international competition and I know that my right hand suddenly appeared to develop St Vitus's dance. With a superhuman effort I directed nineteen shots into the target, but the twentieth, alas, vanished from human ken. It was not a very distinguished performance.

Afterwards Wood, though clearly labouring under strong emotion, was remarkably restrained. I have no doubt, however, that the story of the day's events with which his fellow Marines in England were later regaled would have been worth going a long way to hear. We were a slightly depressed party that evening, for the day's work had lowered the team to sixth place.

The swimming took place in an indoor bath at Hälsingborg at nine o'clock the next evening. The stands were packed with spectators and the water glimmered vivid blue beneath brilliant arc lamps. Each heat consisted of six competitors, and the final placings were done on time; the distance, 300 metres, was twelve lengths of the bath. For those like myself, who prefer that their somewhat laboured strokes should not be witnessed and commented on by a large crowd, this event was also an ordeal.

Swathed in towels, the competitors sat unhappily at the end of the bath until their heat was called. Then pandemonium would break loose in the crowd as they cheered their favourites lining the bath, the cheers rising to a crescendo as the pistol cracked and the swimmers plunged tensely into the water. During the race the enthusiasm would continue, culminating in a roar as the winner touched down. A touch of colour was provided by the Brazilian wives, who, with eyes, teeth and jewels glittering and flashing, would leap to their feet and rend the air with shrieks of *"Madeiros!" "Borges!"*

The Brazilians, Swedes and Americans all swam most impressively. Jack also swam well, into ninth place, and intrigued the crowd by suddenly turning over, swimming at high speed on his back. Jervis, drawn next to the unfriendly Italian, far excelled his normal form in his determination not to be defeated by him, and came well up the list. In my heat I had the mortifying experience, as I completed my eighth length, of hearing the crowd roar applause at a Swede who had in the same time finished the whole twelve. My remaining four lengths passed amid diminished enthusiasm, although the last one witnessed a stirring contest between myself and a Finn who swam the breast-stroke; a battle which I won by a short head. I also beat a Dane, but since he had taken a crashing fall in the riding event and practically lost the use of one arm, it is not a feat I boast about. On the whole, however, the swimming improved our position slightly—our team went up to fifth.

This contest finished very late at night and the running event was at nine-thirty next morning—under twelve hours later. Ominous stories circulated about the two-and-a-half-mile cross-country course; it was said that it was all uphill and that some of the ascents were so steep that you had to go on all fours. The Finns were rubbing their hands; the prospect of a really exhausting run seemed to give them much pleasure. The Italians and Brazilians, on the other hand, looked apprehensive.

Since this was the last event, tension had relaxed and everyone had become less grim. We ran at one-minute intervals—a system which was inevitable since every individual had to be timed, but which I hated because one had to run alone. The only spur, apart from one's own determination, was the hope of catching one or even two competitors who had started earlier, or the fear of being caught up oneself.

Given the opportunity I could have been a useful runner, and I have always been sorry that my obsession with horses before the war prevented me from taking up athletics seriously. Now, however, I was thirty-four, and although still capable of respectable performances, had lost a good deal of speed. I was fit, and on this occasion was determined to push myself to the limit. The course was extremely severe and every hill in the area had been included—the steeper the better. The rumour that some of the inclines required negotiating on all fours was proved to be all too well-founded.

The swimming event only a few hours earlier had taken a good deal out of me, and no doubt I was not the only one affected. It was an exhausting run, of which I remember little except passing an Italian, who shot me a baleful look as I plodded by. Knots of spectators were at every vantage-point, and as I appeared they searched conscientiously in their programmes to identify me so that they could cheer me on in the right language. At last I turned into the long, long straight and there struggling down it was a Brazilian whom I had hoped to pass. I nearly caught him, and then helpers were dumping me on a bank where I reclined until I got my breath back. When the results came through I found I had been tenth, Jack somewhere in the 'teens, and Jervis, who was a first-class runner, third. So he got his Union Jack and *God Save the King* in the end.

The final scores were added up and our team was fourth in the final result. The Swedes, Finns and Brazilians had beaten us with some ease, but we had defeated the French, Americans, Swiss, Danes and Italians. We felt that this on the whole was rather satisfactory, and had a mild celebration. It was a relief once more to be able to take strong drink without feeling guilty of sabotage.

We had a right to be pleased, as it turned out, for sad to say, no British team has subsequently done as well in a World or Olympic Championship. Modern Pentathlon standards have risen steadily in all participating countries, and the sport has been taken up very seriously by Russia and some of the Iron Curtain countries. British standards have also risen considerably, but not in proportion. We usually finish well down the field, and it is obvious that, as in so many sports now, unless a pentathlete dedicates himself completely to his training he has little hope of attaining world class. Given the necessary ability, it is still possible in some sports—athletics for example—to reach world class by training out of working hours. In the case of the Modern Pentathlon, with five events to practise, I believe this is now impossible, and an athlete must be allowed very long periods free from any necessity to earn his living. No Englishman has yet been found both able and willing to dedicate himself so completely as this, and until some are found we must not be disappointed if the British remain a minor Pentathlon nation.

My incursion into the international field showed me that I had reached my Pentathlon peak. If I could have taken indefinite leave for a year with the sole object of training for the 1952 Olympic Games in Helsinki there is little doubt I could still have made the team, but I had other things to do. It was enough, I felt, to have combined my work in the Ministry of Defence with training to international standard for one year in this demanding sport.

I knew I could not repeat this double commitment without one or other suffering, and from every point of view the work was more important. There was no question of any leave for training. I would not struggle on in the Pentathlon at a lower level; it was simply not worth the sacrifice and effort. I had fulfilled an ambition, and now it was time to look for something else. As far as the Pentathlon was concerned, from henceforth I would help others when required, and cheer them on from the ringside.

My decision was not unconnected with the news that I was to return to the Staff College, this time as an instructor. Instructors, as I had earlier discovered, were much freer agents than students. It was clearly high time to return to the race-course.

CHAPTER EIGHT

Steeplechasing Second Wind

ALTHOUGH I sometimes felt, in my more gloomy moments, that as an amateur jockey I was back where I started after the war, this was not really so. I had not been able to ride regularly for some time, but I was remembered occasionally by owners and trainers. Now and again even in this lean period I rode a winner. I was familiar with the steeplechasing world and its personalities, and was by now a reasonably experienced rider.

To gain fresh impetus, however, I needed a horse to replace September Air. This time I was determined to own a top-notcher, and was prepared to wait almost indefinitely until the right one turned up at a price within our means. It took us two years to find the horse we wanted; in the meantime I had to pick up such rides as I could.

One of these rides was the oddest horse I have ever ridden. Everything about it was unexpected. Its name was Ronnie Cronin, but its sex female. In the stable she was like a kindly grandmother; outside she could be a devil. Her eye was gentle and her expression good-natured; but her soft lips concealed a mouth which seemed lined with concrete once it had a bit within it. There were moments when she appeared to go, and probably did go, off her head. These moments were unpredictable and could happen at any time when she was out of the stable, but usually occurred whenever she saw any stretch of grass which tempted her to gallop. Then she would launch herself without any warning into a series of prodigious fly-jumps, standing up on her hind legs and bounding forward like a demented kangaroo. Having completed three or four of these she would have achieved a considerable impetus in whatever direction she had been facing at the time, and there was no chance whatever of stopping her. No gadget and no pair of arms, however strong, could make any impression on her whatever; there was virtually no attainable speed between a trot and a flat-out gallop. She stopped when she felt like it, and there was nothing you could do about it. She was not at all particular where she went, either, and was just as likely to set off through a wire fence as down the gallops.

This would have been intolerable had not her talent for the unexpected included a jumping ability which was both brilliant and safe. She was a useful racehorse and had won several races in Ireland, where she had become a well-known eccentric. Her connections there had, however, withheld any mention of her waywardness when talking to English buyers, and she arrived in England without, so to speak, her crime sheet.

Alec Kilpatrick, who had bought her for Major Freddie Noble, discovered her true form the hard way. On her first morning on the gallops, one of the horses in the string bucked off its rider and made away across Salisbury Plain. Alec was furious. "Give me that old mare," he cried and jumped casually on to Ronnie Cronin's back with intent to pursue. Like a rocket going into orbit she took off and at top speed bore helplessly over the horizon the distinguished trainer, who was not seen again for some considerable time. After that she exercised alone.

It was the task of the stable jockey, Bert Morrow, to introduce her to English race-courses, and he soon discovered that much the most difficult problem was to get her down to the start without first going several times round the course, sometimes in the wrong direction. At Fontwell she completed one circuit before the race had started, and at Worcester she only decided at the very last moment not to take on the River Severn, against which Bert had, in desperation, tried to stop her.

It was at this stage that somebody got the idea of putting up the stable amateur. I was in any case to ride her for Freddie Noble at the end of the season in the Grand Military, and it was thought that I might just as well begin to get used to her at once. From then on I rode her in all her races for the next two seasons.

I was delighted, for she had real potential, provided a way could be found of coping with her tricks. Much the easier part of the problem was the race itself; once launched from the gate she went off like a rocket and all you had to do was guide. She was a patent safety and indeed brilliant jumper despite her craziness, and all the jockey had to do was sit there and be carried round. She had, of course, all the disadvantages of a front runner (a horse which likes to be in front), for very often in the final straight she would run out of steam. Then she would stop very quickly and horses just behind which had been biding their time would swoop upon her and go past. Then the sporting Press would be sure to comment adversely on the incompetent way in which she had been ridden, and on returning to the unsaddling enclosure you were liable to hear remarks like, "Poor thing, made to gallop right out in front like that, no wonder she got beaten!" Sometimes, however, she lasted out and, although her impetuous way of running was a limitation, she began to show promising form.

We developed a technique for getting her down to the start without disaster. We would allow all the other horses to leave the paddock and to canter away down the course. Then I would swiftly mount her and, with attendants hanging on to her bridle as if she were a barrage balloon that had broken loose in a high wind, we would be smuggled rapidly out on to the course. I had then to point her very quickly in the right direction before she did her fly-jump act, and in no time at all we would be galloping frenziedly down towards the start. It was quite useless to try to restrain her, so I would let her gallop like this until the remainder of the field, walking round at the start, came into view. This was the tricky moment, and as we approached them I would throw the reins to her and shout "Whoa!"—for to try to pull her up like a normal horse was to guarantee at least one unauthorised circuit of the course.

This confidence trick was usually successful, or at worst it slowed her up. If she did not come completely to rest she had to be guided against some object too large for her to jump. Most courses possessed a boundary fence which I would have reconnoitred previously and which would serve. Having been brought to a standstill this extraordinary animal would give no more trouble. She would walk round unconcernedly until it was time to start, and then line up as good as gold. The rest was easy.

It was obvious that her jumping ability would sooner or later take her to Aintree, and we decided it would be sooner. First, however, she had to try to win the Grand Military Gold Cup at Sandown Park. Since winning the substitute race on September Air in 1948 I had in the following three seasons been second twice and fourth once in the revived Military Gold Cup, all on different horses, and this time I felt I had a great chance of going one better. My chief obstacle as always at this period was Klaxton and Major David Gibson. Klaxton was a top-class steeplechaser and although a far from easy or predictable ride, usually gave of his best at Sandown. He would idle his way round the first circuit and then, apparently hopelessly tailed off, suddenly condescend to take an interest and loom powerfully out of the blue over the last fence. No one had better reason to know this technique of his than I, for I had already been second to him twice in this race, and it was all too clearly just the technique most liable to upset Ronnie Cronin. All depended on there being no other horse ready to go with her out in front on the first circuit, for if she were allowed to go right out on her own it was beginning to be possible to kid her into a speed rather less than a flat-out gallop and so keep something in reserve. But if another horse came upsides with her she would take it on and run herself, and usually it, out of petrol well before the winning-post, to the joy of those behind.

Unfortunately, in the first circuit of the race events took just the turn I had feared. I was once more treated for the third successive year to the rear view of David Gibson and Klaxton going past the winning-post. Ronnie Cronin's limitations had been exposed again.

Our next engagement was in the Topham Trophy at Aintree, over two and a half miles of the Grand National course. A high-class field had turned out, and we were not given much chance by the Press or the bookmakers. Ronnie Cronin proceeded to give me the best ride I have ever had on any horse in my life. The Aintree fences are some five feet high and she sailed at least six inches over the top of every one. Her jump at Becher's Brook was sensational; she must have cleared it by a foot and although we seemed to be in the air for ten minutes over it, I had never a moment of anxiety. Better still, she was so sobered by the size of the fences that she settled docilely in behind the leading bunch. As we came back on to the race-course proper, with three fences to jump, I found myself gaining on the leaders. In a desperate finish I was beaten into third place, but since the mare was only beaten, at level weights and by a short head, by the horse which was subsequently favourite for the following year's Grand National, we had every reason to be delighted. We wired joyfully to Freddie Noble, at the time steaming back from the Middle East, that he would have a fancied runner for the great Aintree race next year. As Henry Alexander, also an instructor at the Staff College, had won the Aintree Foxhunters at the same meeting we returned to Camberley feeling that the so-called military intelligentsia were not doing too badly and that there was a kick in the old Colonels yet.

As so often happens my expectations for the following season were not fulfilled; indeed they ended in disaster. Ronnie Cronin did herself too well during the summer and came up very gross. She required much work and galloping to become fit for racing, and in the course of this she began occasionally to break small bloodvessels in her nose. Whenever this happened the blood from them would half choke her and bring her to a halt in a way in which no human being ever could. Possibly because of this she became increasingly wild and unpredictable, and I had more and more trouble in getting her down to the start. Her form began to improve after two unsuccessful attempts early in the season and in the New Year we went to Doncaster for a fairly important race.

I had not been to Doncaster race-course since Exercise Turnabout, and my second visit proved to be even less happy than the first. The race was being televised—a matter of some excitement at the Staff College where staff and students, my wife and two infants, were planning to watch me in action. It was, in fact, the television which caused our downfall.

Normally on any race-course you canter down to the start by the shortest way, and rarely is the distance much further than five furlongs. For some reason connected with the television broadcast we were told on this occasion to go the longest way, and so had to cover well over a mile before we arrived at the starting-gate. I had some well-justified forebodings about this arrangement.

Ronnie Cronin gave trouble in the paddock as soon as I mounted her. There was no doubt, I reflected, that this season she was getting wilder every time she ran. With some difficulty we were manœuvred out on to the race-course without an explosion. Then she bounded hysterically into the air and, on landing, galloped off in her usual fashion, as fast as she could lay legs to the ground. I sat still and let her gallop. After she had gone about five furlongs she reduced speed slightly and seemed to look about her, presumably seeking the group of horses which at about this stage she was accustomed to see walking round at the starting-gate. On this occasion they were out of sight about half a mile further on, and she saw nothing. This clearly disconcerted her, but after a slight hesitation her erratic brain supplied her with an answer; she was already racing. She instantly rushed forward again and this time I could tell that she was not going to stop; she had assumed the dogged expression which she wore while racing and which informed those interested that she would neither be pulled up nor passed so long as she had any breath left. I was completely out of control, and knew it.

Back at the Staff College the television audience began to realise that all was not well with their fancy. The commentator must have been relieved to have had this rapidly developing drama with which to fill in the arid period between the horses leaving the paddock and starting the race, and he now began to do the situation justice. A horrified silence fell on the audience, on all, that is, except the two young Blackers who were delighted that their father seemed to be having a lovely gallop. With a trembling hand their mother fed them automatically and abstractedly with chocolate beans.

When the starting-gate and the circling horses came into view, Ronnie Cronin paid not the least attention to them. I went through my entire repertoire. I threw the reins at her, I shouted "Whoa!", I made calming noises at her, all to no avail. She hurtled on past the starting-gate, and there across the course were a steeplechase fence and a hurdle fence side by side and with no way between or round them. Unfortunately they were facing the wrong way for us; they were sloping towards us and not away; in fact, we had to jump one of them backwards. Somewhat naturally

I chose the hurdle. Good jumper as Ronnie Cronin was, she had not expected an obstacle sloping towards her and it tripped her up. With a crash of splintering wood we turned a rapid somersault. I was knocked out, and remained in another world for the next twenty minutes.

I was, however, only flat on my back for a very brief moment. The television viewers, in appalled silence broken by peals of merriment from the two children at seeing Daddy fall off, watched me rise to my feet. A very shaken and unhappy Ronnie Cronin was led up. I mounted her and rode back to the start. I was badly concussed but as always happens when I get a bang on the head, in a belligerent mood. The starter, I later heard on regaining my senses, tried to prevent me from taking part, but was greeted by such a volley of abuse that without further comment he released the starting-gate and let us go. The record books say that we completed the course but were unplaced —not surprisingly. I came to while I was pulling my boots off in the changing-room, and from that day to this the preceding twenty minutes remain a gap in my memory of events.

Ronnie Cronin was withdrawn from circulation for the rest of the season, and was then banished to Scotland. Next year, ridden by Curran, she won several races there before she began once more to get increasingly out of hand. She eventually became too dangerous to ride in public and retired to stud. Even then she did not order her affairs normally; before she could have a foal she died of a twisted gut.

After our fall together I was discovered to have sustained a twisted neck. I had repeated, on a more thorough scale, the dislocation of some vertebrae effected by an earlier fall. After much discussion, I was told firmly by my doctor not to do any more steeplechasing.

This blow was all the harder to bear since we had, some months earlier, found our new steeplechaser. Alec Kil-patrick had arrived back from Ireland with a tall and gangling brown four-year-old which he thought would suit me, although it had only been broken four months before. We went down to his training stable in Wiltshire to see it. It had never raced. Its sire was unfashionable, but the dam made up for this by being bred in the steeplechasing purple. Normally we dither and discuss the pros and cons of buying a horse, particularly when the price is at our limit as this was, but my wife and I were at once agreed. Its name had been registered as Food For Thought, which was obviously impossible. Eventually we reconciled the names of Control, his sire, and Lady Flêche, his dam, into our choice of Pointsman.

This seemed reasonable but what may not, on looking back, have proved reasonable or sensible was the decision we made on his immediate future. Alec Kilpatrick was very understandably determined not to let this promising young horse leave his yard and go off with us to our amateur stable with our inexperienced soldier grooms, to be schooled over jumps and taken hunting. He wanted to run the horse over hurdles during the coming season and teach him how to be a racehorse before he learnt to jump fences. We offered no serious opposition to this very reason-able view, particularly since at that time the horse was of extremely uncertain temper in the stable. On the whole we felt that the strain of having to look after and train this, for us, expensive horse, which Alec had gone to a great deal of trouble to find for us, would be too great, and we agreed that he should begin at once to be trained as a hurdler.

I have often thought since that this was a mistake, though at the time it would have been very hard to have taken the opposite decision. In the event Pointsman gained little from his first season. He was not fully developed and failed to win a hurdle race. He picked up a hit-or-miss style of jumping for which he later became notorious in the steeplechasing world. It was not until many years after this, when he received a thorough jumping education at

home, that he showed that this was not an inevitable state
of affairs. He was not naturally an erratic jumper, but
neither did jumping come naturally to him. He suffered
because he was never in his youth taught the basic lessons
of jumping in slow time. Probably his first season's racing
would have been better spent in the hunting field. But
how easy it is to look back and criticise! If I had taken him
home he might well have slipped up on the road and
broken his leg!

He made his first appearance at Newbury, in a novice
hurdle race, only four months after his arrival in England.
There were some thirty runners in the race and I remember how young and forlorn he looked walking round
the paddock amongst them, neighing anxiously. He spent
most of the race in looking round him and indeed only
started to gallop when the race was half way over, by which
time he was well in the ruck. At the finish he was still
behind but I got off him quite certain that he was a really
good horse. Despite his undistinguished performance, he
had given me the same Bentley-like feel as had Sir John
and the very few other top-class horses which I had ridden.

I rode him in two more hurdle races before my disaster
with Ronnie Cronin. After that, for the first time, I went
racing as an owner and not as a rider, and watched Pointsman ridden by Bert Morrow. After the first shock of re-
adjustment I found, rather to my surprise, that there were
advantages to my changed status. For one thing, I could
enjoy my luncheon. For another, I could remain muffled
in my warm overcoat. I could also (though I tried not to)
make knowing remarks about other people's jockeyship, a
pastime which was altogether too risky while I was still
riding!

The rôle of the owner at a race meeting is thus a comfortable one—comfortable but, I have found, sadly minor.
Naturally, between meetings and during the planning
stage the owners (and their cheque-books) play an indispensable part, but the race and its preliminaries are a com-

bined operation in which only the trainer, the jockey, the horse and its lad have positive rôles. The owner's smart overcoat, his bowler hat, his badge, his knowledgeable conversation, and his favoured position in the paddock can none of them obscure the painful fact that his horse's chance of victory would be in no way impaired if he had remained quietly at home. It is a saddening experience to find oneself thus relegated to the sidelines.

Looking back on past seasons I now realise that I hardly remember the owners for whom I rode; it is the trainers who stand out. It was the trainer who would engage me to ride a certain horse, the trainer for whom I looked on arrival at the meeting and on entering the paddock before the race. Then, from somewhere behind him, he would produce a rather diffident gentleman whom he would introduce as the owner. This gentleman would be allowed to mutter a few words of encouragement, but only until the trainer was ready to deliver himself of his riding instructions. After the race, particularly if unsuccessful, I often never saw the owner at all; he was probably in the bar somewhere muttering about incompetent jockeys. But win or lose I saw the trainer, and it was his words I remembered.

In my riding days (to use a thoroughly middle-aged expression) I always thought that owners must have a very dull time compared with jockeys. Now, though the sensations are quite different, I am not so sure. The jockey on his arrival at the meeting is confronted with a cold and cheerless wait, with neither lunch nor aperitif to prevent his mind from revolving at ever-increasing speed round the forthcoming test. He finds it a relief to be able to change, weigh out, walk to the paddock and mount. By the time he has arrived at the start his anxieties seem to have succumbed to a local anaesthetic which has left his brain clear and his body relaxed. And during the race he is too busy for either excitement or worry.

The owner's feelings travel in almost exactly the reverse

direction. Arriving calm, warm and poised, he attacks an excellent free luncheon and emerges just before the first race in the highest spirits. With what he hopes is a modest but quietly confident air he informs enquiring friends of the well-being of his horse and advises them to have a "bit on". This happy phase lasts till about half an hour before his horse's race. Then, like the biting, insistent little wind which warns the skier that he has sat too late in the Alpine sunshine, niggling doubts begin to trickle into his mind. Is his horse really as good as he thinks? Is not the opposition really far too strong, despite his trainer's assurances? Are not the sporting Press sure to make wounding references to it in the morning papers? Might it not fall? Or even hurt itself, or the jockey? As these questions loom larger in his mind the owner's confident air begins to evaporate and he falls silent.

Those who own a large string of horses are probably immune to these feelings, but for one whose hopes (and spare cash) centre round one horse only the whole occasion has begun to matter far too much. The jockey has other rides, the trainer other charges, but many owners have no other horse. For them the stakes are high.

In the paddock before the race it is sometimes difficult to make the cheerful conversation which the occasion demands. The jockey appears and the trainer usually cracks a joke to relieve the tension—the more futile the better. Once Alec could not be in the paddock and the onus of making this joke fell on me. I am no good at that sort of thing and nothing came; we stood—a gloomy and silent little group—in the middle of the paddock until it was time to mount.

When the horses leave the paddock the trainer, having given his final instructions, becomes as powerless to influence events as the owner. Together they move pensively towards the stand, feeling like a General who has just hurled his last armoured division into the battle and is hastening to a viewpoint to watch its progress. Assuming a frozen smile to mask the fact that he has a bad attack of jitters, the owner stares through quivering binoculars at the scene below him. In the *mêlée* of the race he is constantly losing or mistaking his colours—now he locates them right up in front, next a long way behind. For half a mile he watches the wrong horse struggling in rear, then loses it altogether and with a gasp of relief finds the right one with the leaders. He discovers that his colours, so proudly worn by himself in previous seasons, consist of a combination which is quite invisible at long range. As the race reaches its climax, the crowd around begin to shout, but he, if his horse is in any way concerned with the finish, becomes rigid and silent with tension. As the horses pass the post a tidal wave of relief or disappointment passes over his head, but at least he is able to relax, and he then finds that he has not only practically lost the use of his legs but also most of the power of speech.

So, to my surprise, I did not find it dull to be an owner, and when Pointsman in his second season graduated to novice steeplechases it became very exciting. By February he had won four races and was being hailed as a coming star. The chief blemish on his reputation was his jumping. He found it very difficult to adjust his long, loping stride on meeting his fences. If he met them in stride he would outjump all his rivals and gain at least a length; if he met a fence out of stride he would hit it hard and lose more ground than he had gained. He had an acrobatic facility for retaining his legs in a crisis, and the jockey needed, on occasions, to be an acrobat too if he was to remain in place. Bert had brought off one or two incredible recoveries during the season, but once or twice even his adhesive properties had been defeated.

The Grand Military Gold Cup was in March; Pointsman was, of course, entered. Who was to ride him? It had to be a serving officer. I could think of no one who would suit this brilliant but still very inexperienced horse. In any case, it was one thing to watch a professional jockey riding my horse, and quite another to select an amateur of whose ability I might not be certain. I knew quite well what the answer to this one was, but first a little brainwashing had to be done to wife and trainer. They were eventually convinced that, with the best chance we ever had of winning this elusive prize, I should disobey doctors and ride Pointsman myself.

Klaxton had by now retired, but the 1954 Grand Military Gold Cup was none the less a vintage race. Pointsman was one of the best young steeplechasers of the time, and another young horse, called Roughan, ridden by Philip Fielden, later won many races including the Topham Trophy at Liverpool. Point of Law, ridden by Michael Gordon Watson, was more mature than either of his two young opponents and had been a regular winner in Ireland. The rest of the field was less distinguished.

I suppose that I was by some way the most experienced rider in the field but I had not ridden in a race for fifteen months, and had never before been on Pointsman's back in a steeplechase. He was looking light after a hard season and had obviously passed his best for the year; his jumping ability was suspect. It was therefore remarkable, and dismaying, to find ourselves hot favourites at very nearly even money. I let my stirrups down to a most un-jockey-like length, determined that whatever else I did, I would not fall off. To have been second in this race three times running was bad enough; to part company unnecessarily on my last appearance, and from my own horse, would be too much.

There were eleven runners, and we surged forward over the first fence uneventfully. Pointsman got unbalanced going round the first bend and made an error which cost us some ground. Down the back straight we settled down in our new partnership. He was jumping perfectly and as we turned back past the stands to complete our first circuit his powerful stride had taken us up into third place. No horse of any consequence was in front of us, however, and our two dangers, Roughan and Point of Law, were close up behind and biding their time. We turned away from the stands and, as always at Sandown, took advantage of the slight downhill gradient to start racing in earnest.

Pointsman was still in third place a mile from home, but then came crisis number one. We galloped into a plain fence right out of stride. First he decided to stand right off it and reach for it, and then with no warning at all he changed his mind. He took another stride and appeared to dive clean through the fence about a foot from the bottom. For a split second there was no horse in front of me at all; all I saw was the grass lurching past me below—and one long brown leg appearing from nowhere to save us from crumpling to earth. I clutched everything I could see, mane, reins, saddle, neck, and by some miraculous means regained the saddle. We were by then last, and the wind was knocked out of Pointsman. I restrained myself from pressing him on too suddenly but with two remarkable leaps and with his formidable stride again in full working order he pulled the leaders back until, as we began the turn into the final straight, we hit the front. Then Roughan, with Philip Fielden sitting ominously still, galloped easily past us and took a two-length lead. Point of Law loomed up alongside. I began to feel uneasy.

The third fence from home is called the Pond fence, because there is a small pool near it. Coming into it the three horses were well clear of the rest, and Pointsman was closing slightly on Roughan. I drove him into the fence and he made there the worst mistake I have ever experienced without total disaster. There was a thudding jolt and crackle of birch; again I seemed to be tumbling over a precipice yawning below me; the reins tore through my hands as if the world's biggest salmon were hooked to their end. Frantically I clung. Once more when all seemed lost, disaster was averted by that long, brown leg which again appeared from nowhere. As he recovered, Pointsman's nose (according to several spectators) literally touched the grass. By the time we had staggered upright again and our composure was restored, we were nearly at a standstill. Several lengths ahead Roughan and Point of Law were galloping in to the penultimate fence. We could hardly be better than third.

Amid my despair a violent spasm of determination took hold of me. I had not felt like this since I had so surprised Rareweed before that deadheat long ago. I gathered Pointsman together and hurled him forward in pursuit. It looked quite hopeless, until I began to realise what a tremendous horse I was riding.

Pointsman was, at the time, a comparatively undeveloped six-year-old and had a hard season. In this race he had made two mistakes, either of which would have been disastrous to a normal horse, and which had lost him a conservative twenty lengths. In a quarter of a mile, starting from virtually a standstill, he had to overtake two good horses which had a lead of six lengths on him or more. He lowered his head and dourly extended his stride as he battled up the Sandown hill.

Coming in to the penultimate fence, which he jumped superbly, he had cut down the distance to four lengths and, ridiculously, I began to hope. I thought I could detect signs that the well-known Sandown gradient was beginning to have its effect on the two leaders. They began to weaken very slightly, and they both came away from the rails into the middle of the course, intent on their duel. Pointsman and I, ravenous for every inch of ground, hugged the rails, and as we rode into the last fence we were only a length behind.

Everything depended on this last fence and only desperate measures would be enough. I could feel that we were hopelessly out of stride and all set for another ghastly error. The only chance was for him to stand off practically outside the wings and reach for it; if he tried to take another stride as he had already done twice before, we were finished. He rose magnificently to the occasion. Few people can have appreciated what it cost this young horse, by now very tired, to put everything to the touch as he proceeded to do. He did the only thing which could possibly have won us the race, and no jockey could have made him do it; it was his own decision, welling up instinctively from the fighting intelligence which only good thoroughbreds have. He unleashed a rocketing bound which carried us a length past the two leaders, and after a desperate struggle up the straight, past the post. By a neck.

This story-book finish, rounded off by the presentation of the Grand Military Gold Cup by the Queen Mother was the end of my active racing career—if you can call it that, for it had been too interrupted and in many ways unsatisfactory to merit the name. You should start racing young, when commitments, business or family, are less constricting. I made what I could of my late start and I would not have missed a minute of my steeplechasing. Even the Ronnie Cronin disaster was well worth enduring for the magnificent ride she gave me at Aintree. Steeplechasing consists of ups and downs, and in my experience you often gain as much from the downs as from the ups. It is a magnificent sport.

Soon after my win at Sandown I went north to command my regiment, and I then parted with Pointsman to our friends Sir Percy and Lady Orde, who also at that time owned the great 'chaser Galloway Braes. After a brilliant career marred only by his jumping, and during which he at times ranked as perhaps the best in England or Ireland, Pointsman strained a tendon and came back to us.

Since his return, having been schooled over showjumps by my wife, he has won two more steeplechases and a point-to-point, bringing his winning total up to twenty races. Rising twelve he ran Mandarin to a short head in the King George VI Steeplechase at Kempton Park, and in the following year he won a number of showjumping competitions. I have hunted the Staff College Draghounds off his back. There is no more versatile horse than the Irish thoroughbred, as I later found with Workboy!

My active steeplechasing was finished, but my future showjumping partner was still racing. In any case, serious showjumping had not yet entered into my calculations, and was not to do so for another two years. In the meantime, other horizons beckoned.

CHAPTER NINE

"Why Don't You Try Oils?"

DURING our stay in London we spent a good deal of our spare time wandering round picture galleries. Many of the works of art which we saw filled me with wonder that anyone could conceive and execute such marvels of composition, colour and technique. At the other end of the scale we saw paintings on exhibition which were often charming but which, it seemed to me, could not have required an impossibly high standard of skill to execute.

I became more and more fascinated by the problem of painting pictures. Did one have to have some special talent, or could anyone, without aspiring to a work of art, produce a bearable painting? In my drawing lessons at school I had shown neither interest nor talent in the rendering of the inevitable groups of boxes, and had hardly reached the stage of painting anything. On the other hand I had found from experience that where there's a will there's a way.

There is nothing, Heaven knows, unusual in taking up painting as an amateur. Indeed it is a highly fashionable hobby now. Even so, people obviously think it rather odd that someone active in sport should paint, and conclude that I must have some special talent which makes it all come easily to me. This conclusion, as this chapter will show, is wide of the mark. The sportsman cannot always be active—at least if he tries to be he will sooner or later become an intolerable bore. He is wise to cultivate sedentary hobbies and interests. I, at least, have found that someone who cannot draw, and whose knowledge of painting has been gleaned from art galleries and conversations with friends, is capable of having great fun with brush and canvas. He may not paint good pictures, indeed a great many will be intolerable, but he will, if I am any guide, produce an occasional result which will please himself if no one else. This is a very satisfactory experience.

I started rather dubiously with a small box of oil-paints, and several books of instruction. The latter I soon decided were a dead loss. The eminent authors had for the first few pages made a stern effort to talk in simple terms, but then, like Ronnie Cronin, they had got the bit between their teeth and were away at full gallop. Chroma Scales, Colour Notation, Scumbling, Pyramids of Stability and many other daunting technical terms swam before me. It appeared that I had a year's work in front of me before I could begin to paint; I had to make scales for Colour, Hue, Value, Chroma and Temperature respectively before apparently it was safe to start at all. I was unable to understand all this, and was not prepared to try. I flung the books aside. I went to the larder and fetched an orange, which I put on a white plate.

There was the orange; there was the plate. The one, obviously, must be painted orange, the other white. First one drew the outlines, not very accurately, but well enough. To produce an orange colour one must mix yellow and red, and lighten the mixture with some white. One side of the subject was more shaded than the other; a darker colour, perhaps brown, should be applied. The oils were nice to work with, if rather messy; one colour could be dabbed over the other and the whole lot scraped off if necessary— much easier than water-colour. I very soon struck the obvious difficulty—I could mix an orange colour but not *the* orange colour; I could not match the hue to the subject.

Perhaps if I added a little blue . . . Gradually a recognisable but unappetising image was produced.

In succeeding weeks I tried other still-life objects, attempting to copy on canvas the exact shades and colours I observed in them, and then rushing off to the National Gallery or the Tate to see how the great masters had dealt with the same objects. I found that to achieve a reasonable result I had to be painstaking and persevering; the more trouble I took, the better the result. My lack of drawing ability was annoying but not fatal; the rules of perspective are, after all straightforward, and if you intend subsequently to cover the drawing with paint, it does not much matter if you make a mess with a rubber first.

On the whole I was encouraged by my early efforts, and more and more intrigued by the problems of painting. It was time, I felt, to seek outside advice. I had not the opportunity nor the time, to join a class at an art school. Organised instruction is obviously necessary for those who are to paint for a livelihood, but not, I am sure, for the amateur. Let him "be himself", as a wise man once advised me, uninfluenced by instructors or schools of thought. I took my work to Mr William T. Wood in Chelsea, a most charming and distinguished old man of talent, who would criticise kindly but firmly, make a number of most helpful suggestions, and would sometimes let me watch him paint a picture. From conversations with him I gained many of the essentials which otherwise I would not have grasped so soon or so clearly, and much stimulation of thought.

Gradually, in the course of several visits, certain rules became clearer to me; the importance of tone value—the strength, regardless of hue, of one colour compared to the one next to it—the green tree, for instance, against the blue sky; the fact that the farther away a colour is the fainter, the "bluer" its colour; the meaning of composition. These rules, I found, were much easier to state than to obey, but at least they provided a proposition which one can recognise and grapple with, a definite target at which to aim. The closer I obeyed these rules, the better the result. Nothing magical here, you will note; no great talent required, simply toil, sweat and tears.

With mounting excitement I discovered that the door which I had timidly pushed open actually led somewhere. I bought bigger canvases, bigger brushes and more paint. I had some of my pictures framed, discovered how much the framing improved them, and how important it is to go to an expert framemaker. I already knew from my visits to innumerable galleries what style of painting I admired, and I soon discovered that as a subject buildings attracted me most. I found it fascinating to plan the picture from the first tentative charcoal mark on the virgin canvas to the completed work. As Winston Churchill has noted, the process is not unlike the direction of a battle. So often, with two-thirds of the picture painted, defeat stares you in the face; the canvas is dull and lifeless when by that time it should be starting to live. But if you have planned aright you have kept in reserve some final strokes of brighter colour which, judiciously placed at the critical moment, may pull the whole engagement out of the fire. Planning, perseverance, and then boldness of execution are the qualities needed—perhaps that is why so many successful Generals are good painters too.

Gradually my pictures went up on our walls, and later the occasional one or two were even accepted for exhibition. Some of the early ones, before I became more discriminating, were horrors and I can never admire sufficiently the tact and self-control of our visitors, suddenly confronted by these peculiar objects. I discovered, too, that the painter is completely blind to the faults of any picture which he has just created. It is rather like, in your bachelor days, having an unsuitable girl-friend; you defend your new acquisition passionately against the strictures of your friends and relatives, and think you have never seen anything so wonderful. But its charm, like hers, tends to wane; you begin to notice that in certain lights it

(Above) Receiving a prize from Prince Bernhard of the Netherlands, Chile 1959.

(Below) On tour with the C.I.G.S., 1959. With the U.S. army at Fort Benning, Georgia.

The Blacker-Workboy partnership in action at an English show.

Before a parachute jump.

does not look too good; there is occasionally a certain coarseness in the features and a stridency in its appeal; and then one day in a terrible unguarded moment you wonder why on earth you ever took up with it. It goes out of your life, replaced by a new favourite. No room for sentiment here.

There are minor drawbacks, I found, which the amateur painter must accept from the moment he first puts brush to canvas. For example, it takes very little to make one's female relations and acquaintances start saying in awed tones, "Of course, my dear, you know he *paints*?" It is then not long before people start asking your opinion of their pictures "as an expert", and beseeching you to tell them whether their Raeburn should be cleaned or not, and if so which firm you recommend.

Another drawback, which may not affect some painters but which I shall always find disconcerting when at work is the deep interest which my figure crouched over the canvas inspires in passers-by. From this point of view it is unlucky that I like painting buildings. I often envy those who prefer still-life, or interiors, portraits or views of wild and uninhabited places.

When the average passer-by notices a painter at work, he generally reacts in one of three ways. Those who are least busy or least inhibited adopt the first and most obvious course; as if drawn by an invisible string they take up positions in rear of the painter and remain there until their curiosity is satisfied. They discuss the picture amongst themselves, sometimes in wounding terms.

Those in the next category cannot bring themselves to be quite so blatant, but are determined to have a look all the same. They generally feign a deep interest in a neighbouring shop window, and, executing a wide, turning movement, gradually manœuvre themselves into visual range of their target.

The third category comprises those whose self-discipline is such that they are able to resist the temptation, and with

E

firm tread and set features march steadily by. It also includes such acquaintances of the painter who suspect that they may have met this scruffy-looking object somewhere before, but are determined not to give the fact away.

Children are far more predictable; they all belong to the first category. With wild shouts of, "Look, look, here's an artist!" they rush to the scene with such excited and amazed expressions that you might think a wild baboon was loose in the streets. Once in position behind the painter they keep up a continuous running commentary. They are a mercifully uncritical audience; if they can recognise, however dimly, the object being painted, they go into transports of delight, and encourage the artist with cries of "Ooh, isn't it luvly!" or "I do wish I could dror like that!" This involves little strain on the painter, but it becomes more trying when they start asking questions of the type of: "Where do you live, Artist?" and "How much will you sell it for, Artist?" It is difficult to strike the right note; any attempt to answer them inevitably means laying down one's brush and embarking on a long and confused conversation, and yet one does not like to be rude. I generally adopt the abstracted air of one who is completely lost in his art, and grunt non-committally whenever a child becomes unusually insistent.

This detached attitude cannot always be maintained. Once, when I had been foolish enough to park myself near a village school, I was soon surrounded by a crowd about ten deep. Those at the back could not see satisfactorily, so pushed, and those in front were soon in attitudes which reminded me of the police keeping the fans off Miss Elizabeth Taylor. While the mass panted to and fro, the usual babel of comments arose from it. "This is the first artist I've seen," said one little boy excitedly. " 'Tisn't the first I've seen," said a little girl squashingly. "One of my mistresses, Miss Sims, is an artist." This remark focussed the crowd's attention upon her. "Is she a better artist than this one?" they enquired with interest. "Miss Sims," said the little girl, diplomatically steering her way between the horns of her dilemma, "paints *differently*." Just as I was thinking that here was a girl with a future, a small child was projected violently forward into my palette, and I had to break the gathering up.

Even within the family circle the painter's concentration is sometimes broken, particularly if his family is young. One afternoon soon after I began to paint I was finishing off a picture in the garden, when round the corner, just returned from a picnic, came our two small children and the Peke. They stood for a moment in respectful silence, but finally the elder said, "Oh, look, there's a poor fly stuck in the paint—do let me get it out." And with that he plunged his finger into my picture and emerged with the fly and a coating of blue and white cloud effect. As I was testily wiping his fingers, the younger child somehow got some large blobs of red and yellow paint on his hand, which, with the gesture apparently automatic to young male children, he immediately wiped on his jersey. Impelled by cries of maternal rage, I set my palette on the ground and led him down the path to the potting-shed, there to apply the necessary aids. When I got back I found the Peke had meanwhile sat down and scratched itself in the centre of my palette, and now, with its behind sporting every colour of the rainbow, was marching off to repeat the operation on the drawing-room carpet.

"Happy are the painters," writes Sir Winston Churchill, "for they shall not be lonely." Here is yet another of this great man's remarks with which I unreservedly agree.

CHAPTER TEN

The Amateur Journalist

ONCE upon a time I used to write frivolous sporting articles for what was in other respects an intellectual weekly. When that magazine came under more serious-minded management this journalistic outlet ceased, and others have only operated in occasional spurts since that day. Even so, amongst other events I can say that I have reported two Grand Nationals, the French and the English, at Auteuil and Aintree.

Of the two occasions, I look back on the Auteuil expedition with by far the greater pleasure. My visit was in the nature of a return trip, for in 1945 I had taken part there in a contest known as the *Steeple-Chase des Alliés*. I had greatly enjoyed this experience, although there must be few sports which lend themselves so ill to international competition as steeplechasing. The race had been confined to Allied officers and sponsored by *Le Club de Gentleman-Riders*, which had in its innocence assumed that if you were an officer you were automatically an amateur. It had reckoned without the methodical processes of the British demobilisation programme, which enabled the cunning English to arrive with a team of six, two of whom were undeniably officers, gentlemen, riders—but none the less professional, indeed no less a pair than Captain Bryan Marshall and Captain Jack Bissill. This had caused a mild crisis, but by far the most vexed question which had arisen on that occasion was the provision of horses. We had come to Paris on the understanding that the various French owners, in the interests both of inter-Allied solidarity and of the large amount of stake-money involved, would rally round and provide us with adequate mounts. The attitude of these good men had, however, been much influenced by a similar contest held previously at Marseilles. Here the riders had drawn their horses by lot, and the favourite, a valuable and mettlesome animal, had been secured by a large and not very competent Russian. The owner had at once scratched his horse, but the inter-Allied temperature had then risen so high that he had been forced to re-enter it. The ensuing race had not been the success that had been hoped, and afterwards it had been generally conceded that owners would in future select their own "gentlemen-riders".

Thus the reserve displayed by *Le Club* towards our two professionals had been by no means shared by the owners, who fell upon them with cries of delight and quickly supplied them with such horses as had not already been claimed by the French competitors. At the same time it became painfully clear to our four amateurs that unless they looked after their own interests they were in danger of being left out in the cold. For three days there was consequently a gentlemanly but none the less determined free-for-all, from which I emerged with an animal of modest ability but guaranteed to jump the course. I have forgotten its name but not its breeding, which was down on the race-card as *"Ginger-Ale et Goody"*. Thus I made acquaintance with Auteuil.

French fences are built on a different principle from British. Ours are sloping, comparatively stiff and made of birch; theirs are upright, soft, and made mostly of privet hedge. British trainers and jockeys devote much time and energy towards ensuring that their horses, when confronted by an obstacle, jump over the top; the French consider it absurd to do this when it is so much quicker to go through the fence half-way up. So it is—over a French fence. This different approach explains why French and English steeplechasers do not visit each other's countries so frequently or so successfully as their flat-racing relations.

The authorities at Auteuil, however, are not so unenterprising as to restrict the hazards to mere privet hedges. There is *la rivière*, a forbidding-looking water jump. There is what my newspaper called *"le terrible rail-ditch and fence, énorme haie précédée d'un tronc d'arbre et d'un fossé"*. There is *le bullfinch*, a hedge about six feet tall through which the horses are expected to burst their way, and to add variety there are a great many little white posts and rails, arranged at odd intervals rather in the style of a *Concours Hippique*.

There is a pleasantly light-hearted air about a French race-meeting. You pay very much less to go in than you do in England, and once inside you are not herded into separate enclosures according to the amount you have paid. It does not apparently in the least matter if the races start half an hour late, and the general public mills happily about amongst the horses, protesting volubly if a hoof whistles too close past their ears, but otherwise displaying the same indifference to peril as they do in the streets.

There were nine starters for the Grand Steeple-Chase that year. Most of them were small, full of quality, and would have looked far more at home at Ascot than Aintree. In particular did this apply to the favourite, Fifrelet, which was reputed to have won its last five races *"avec une facilité déconcertante"*. Tournay, winner of the previous year, was more imposing, but the horse in which I was principally interested was the good English 'chaser Glen Fire, third favourite for our Grand National. He was ridden here by Michael Scudamore.

While the horses were walking out, my party was wafted up in a lift to a roomy balcony overlooking the course, where we found reserved seats, an attractive-looking bar and an air of spacious ease. The horses paraded below us, cantered down to the start and, after a pause, were off. For a moment I was so enchanted by the scene that I forgot to notice what was happening in the race. The expanse of grass below us, well watered, was a vivid summer green, set off by the neat privet hedges, white rails and brilliant trees. The sun poured down on gay dresses, flowers, the colours of the jockeys and the glossy coats of the nine galloping thoroughbreds. When the field, tightly packed together, took off and hung poised at full stretch above the wide water jump, it was perfection.

When my attention returned to the race, I saw that Fifrelet was skimming along in front, apparently able to judge the exact height below which each fence became too stiff for safety. The rest followed in a bunch just behind him. Glen Fire did not appear to be enjoying himself much; the white rails, the whitewashed mud wall and *le bullfinch* all surprised him considerably. He jumped higher and more deliberately at every fence, and gradually his attitude became one of undisguised suspicion. Fifrelet purred smoothly along in front, with the crowd beginning to shout him home. Then, at the second-from-last fence, he made his only error. For a second he struggled valiantly to regain his feet, failed, and turned a complete somersault. As the winner, a horse named Pharamond, passed the post, I noticed that Glen Fire had decided against jumping *le bullfinch* for the second time.

It had been an entertaining, relaxed day, and as I was writing for a weekly I was able to go home and compose my report in slow time.

Far different was my Aintree experience in journalism, some years later. One day, right out of the blue, I was asked to report the Grand National for the *Sunday Times*. The regular correspondent was ill and, remembering my racing articles in the weekly which had by then disowned me, he had suggested my name as his replacement. This was a shock to me but after the minimum of thought I accepted. It would be, I thought, rather faint-hearted to refuse and no doubt I would struggle through somehow.

It gradually occurred to me that there is a world of difference between the composition of an article in slow time and journalism proper, which in this case involved telephoning my account to the newspaper some ninety minutes after the end of the race. During this brief period I would have to make certain what had happened in the race, interview the principal characters and then compose an account of sufficient penetration, accuracy and wit to satisfy the readers of the *Sunday Times*. I could only think of two things to do to speed things up: to learn all the jockeys' colours and to memorise the horses' numbers. The first precaution was sensible, but the second was a total failure; I took the numbers from the list of runners in *Sporting Life* and, on the day, one horse withdrew. All the numbers below nine thereupon moved up one, which naturally was no help at all.

The 1955 Grand National was the wettest on record. Indeed, if it had been any other race it would probably have been cancelled, such was the waterlogged state of the course. The rain deluged down without respite and an air of gloom enveloped the whole assembly. I slopped about trying to find the Press Room, past groups of unhappy race-goers crouching under the nearest available shelter, and eventually found Peter Willett of the *Sunday Graphic*. As I was temporarily an employee, like him, of Lord Kemsley, he had been instructed to show the new boy the ropes.

The ropes consisted of a large room filled with telephones and an interviewing room downstairs. My bear-leader told me not to waste time in the interviewing room —"All they do there is ask the owner's wife about her hats and how often she's been married." The real interviewing apparently was a matter of private enterprise, a question of seeking out the leading characters and extracting "copy" from them. To my intense relief, I then heard of the wonders of Associated Press, an organisation with

agents deployed at every key point and capable of supply-
ing information to the slowest journalist at a moment's
notice. I was fairly sure I should need A.P.

Mrs Topham is, we know, a busy woman and I do not
suppose she will ever have time to do anything about the
Press Stand at Aintree, but all the same it leaves a great
deal to be desired. It is simply a slab of concrete, with no
nonsense about overhead cover, still less anything to write
on. Its sole concession to inclement weather is a large piece
of plate glass down the left-hand side, but as rain makes it
as impossible to see through this glass as it is to see through
a windscreen with a broken wiper, only the more uninterested journalists were availing themselves of its shelter.
The rest of us, poising our pencils expectantly over sodden
race-cards, stood in the open waiting for the race to start.

As the horses departed into the driving rain it became
increasingly impossible to see what was going on. By the
time they reached Becher's I might as well have been on
the moon for all I could have told anyone about the race
so far. Peter O'Sullevan, of the *Sunday Express,* who has
X-ray eyes, proclaimed that Sundew was leading and
named the second and third. Convulsively, I bent down
to make a note, whereupon a pint of water from my bowler
deluged down on to my race-card and reduced it to pulp.
I threw it to the floor, realising that memory alone would
have to serve.

But by the end of the race I had not much to remember.
I knew the rough order in which they passed the stands
the first time and I could have told you the first ten to
finish, but otherwise my main feeling as I descended was
that something would have to be done extremely quickly.
I forced my way through the mass of ecstatic Irishmen
who were capering about round the unsaddling enclosure
and went in search of someone to interview. Mr Vincent
O'Brien, the winning trainer, is used to winning the
Grand National, and spoke so quietly and calmly that I,
well at the back, could not hear what he said. Mr Phonsy

O'Brien, his brother, was more animated, but I only arrived in time for the tail-end of his remarks. During the next half hour I realised that I might as well have taken on Stirling Moss in a *Grand Prix* as try to beat my fellow journalists to an interview. The moment a suitable target emerged from the dressing-room he was instantly swarmed upon, three deep, and I, faint but pursuing, could only catch the occasional muttered word. As foreseen, I fell gratefully back on Associated Press.

By a quarter to five I dared wait no longer. I had three-quarters of an hour in which to compose and telephone through a piece worthy of the *Sunday Times,* and no coherent sentence had yet entered my head. As I went through the Press Room door Peter Willett came out and his look told me that the readers of the *Sunday Graphic* had already been catered for. I sat down by a telephone, drew up some foolscap and, like everyone else in the room, began desperately to scribble.

As time wore on it became more and more like an examination at which one is not doing well. Twenty minutes to go and still only a quarter of the piece written. Sweat slowly gathers on the brow. More and more of one's fellow scribblers rise, collect their belongings and sweep disdainfully out. Slowly the room empties. But, unlike an exam, there is all this shouting into the telephone, which distracts the attention in the frantic hope that some pearl may be overheard and used. But all one hears is the representative of the *Sunday Pictorial* sobbing that "the Queen's smile warmed the chilled hearts of the drenched Aintree thousands", which is really not much good to the *Sunday Times.*

At last I was left alone in the room with one other sufferer, and at a quarter to six I was able to raise the telephone and send through an account which sounded, and was, singularly unimpressive. But by then I was thankful to send anything through. A look of anguish passed over the face of my defeated rival across the room as I rose to go and, face twitching, he cried pleadingly, "Before you go, for God's sake what was the third?"

I stumbled out into the rain, badly in need of a drink. Aintree looked just like a dance hall that had closed. The usually jovial barmaid was reacting from the efforts she had made to smile during the day and was enjoying the luxury of being thoroughly disagreeable. She would not give me any whisky, or indeed anything except a piece of her mind. So I left, wet, tired and not at all happy about the probable reaction at thousands of breakfast tables to my journalistic efforts. But I need not have worried. That night the newspapers went on strike and no breakfast table got anything at all. And, as far as the readers of the *Sunday Times* were concerned, it was probably just as well.

CHAPTER ELEVEN

Showjumping Prelude

I STARTED my showjumping young, as do most children brought up with ponies. Indeed at the age of thirteen I had the honour of becoming first jockey to Mr Phil Oliver, in days long before the appearance of sons Alan and Paul in this world. His pony was called Tipover, and must have been almost the founder member of the formidable string which dominated English showjumping in the early nineteen-fifties. But as a schoolboy away for most of the year at boarding-school, it was impossible, even under his professional eye, to take showjumping seriously.

Olympia and Richmond were the two shows which stood head and shoulders in prestige above all others. They took place, annoyingly enough, in termtime, and my schoolmasters were unsympathetic over the question of letting me off to ride there. Consequently I never saw the great military riders in action in the 'twenties and early 'thirties, and my idea of adult showjumping was culled exclusively from the open events at the local county shows. These did not provide a spectacle likely to instil in anyone's breast a burning enthusiasm for the sport.

A course of at the most eight obstacles would be erected —one cannot say laid out—in the ring. There would be a bush fence, gate, stile, wall, rail—all upright—and a triple bar. At the grander shows there would be an "in and out", consisting of two upright fences, and a water jump. On the top rail of each fence would be laid a thin slither of wood called a lathe, which could nearly be dislodged by the wind of a hoof passing close to it and which counted half a fault if it fell.

Competitors and their horses provided a sight even stranger to modern eyes than the fences. At most shows riders wore what they pleased, and many appeared in the ring clothed in cloth caps and jodhpurs, with horses' heads secured firmly in one position with a very short martingale. The horses themselves were usually heavy and common; many of hackney breeding with little docked tails. Horse and rider were trained and turned out, not unnaturally, for the task before them, the negotiation of very flimsy, upright obstacles in their own time. They would crawl round the course until the water jump impended; then they would halt at the end of the ring and fumble with their martingales. Having freed the horses' heads they would hurtle dramatically at the water jump and disappear out of the ring in a cloud of dust, after which they would lash their horses' heads down again in preparation for the jump-off. Jump-offs went on interminably and were never decided on time.

I took a mild interest in these contests, but how could they compare with the glamour of steeplechasing in the Golden Miller, Easter Hero, Gregalach era? Local point-to-points, too, were far more exciting; so was pursuit of the Bicester hounds in full cry across that then unspoilt country. In this I shared the feelings of the vast majority of horsemen and horsewomen at that time. Showjumping was all very well for Weedon-trained officers who had a chance of jumping abroad, and for a few professionals, but the enthusiasm which fills the novice jumping classes today with vast throngs from all walks of life is a modern phenomenon.

When the officers of the 5th Inniskilling Dragoon Guards returned to the regiment in 1946 from their various wartime posts, it was under the command of Colonel Alec Scott. With Colonel Mike Ansell, also a member of the regiment, he had been in the pre-war British showjumping team, and was determined that our reputation as a showjumping regiment should be enhanced. In this he succeeded admirably. He and Arthur Carr very soon became members of the reconstituted British team, and Arthur earned a Bronze Medal in the 1948 Olympic Games. On a lower level than these two prominent horsemen, the regiment owned a flourishing second eleven of showjumping officers, of which I soon found myself one. All this activity depended, as indeed did a large part of the British team at the time, on captured German showjumpers.

On my return I was out of tune with this concentration on showjumping. I was what pre-war officers called a "racing swine" and my thoughts were occupied largely with the 1948 Grand National. When this, and the other matters which filled that, for me, hectic spring were dealt with, an attempt was made to subvert the racing swine. I was allocated a German showjumping mare called Sarah and told to get on with it.

Sarah had done little jumping of recent years because James Whetstone, from whom I inherited her, had considered himself too heavy. He was, however, a very fine horseman and had schooled her to a high standard on the flat. I soon found that not only had I been lucky in this respect, but that in the distant past Sarah had learnt a great deal about jumping too. Thanks to James Whetstone she was extremely easy to ride, was most careful and co-operative, and possessed a big jump. I found that, although I was apt to adopt a racing seat in absent-minded moments, I was the fortunate possessor of a reasonably good eye for judging my stride into a fence.

German shows in those days were not German shows, they were shows held in Germany and run by the British Army of the Rhine. There were no German competitors and, with the opposition reduced by the absence of various officers training for the 1948 Olympics, Sarah and I had a successful season. We ended it by winning the chief individual prize in Cologne, despite the presence of a civilian British team and a French team. To show that despite all this subversion I was still a racing swine, I next day flew back to ride Sir John at the October Cheltenham meeting. We were beaten by a short head, and I just missed an unusual double.

The Staff College swept me away from Sarah, who could undoubtedly have made her mark at the White City had the opportunity offered. Military duties lightened by steeplechasing and the Pentathlon claimed me and I thought no more of showjumping for a while. Two incidents, however, in 1949 sent their messages winging into the future.

One August morning I played truant from the Staff College, and rode out with the Kilpatrick string. August is a particularly interesting time to ride with a string of steeplechasers, to cast your eye over the newcomers and estimate which in the coming season will turn out to be swans, and which geese. At the back of the string there jiggled and bounced three brand new four-year-olds from Ireland. They made no particular impression on me as I looked them over, though they should have. I saw no indication that the obstreperous brown youngster by Steel Point would one day become second favourite for a Grand National, and even less that the other brown, a quieter, less positive character, was to become the great Galloway Braes, winner on many famous occasions and still holder of the Kempton Park three-mile record. The third youngster, the excitable little black horse bringing up the rear, was called Workboy.

The string wound its way through the Wiltshire woods, appeared at the bottom of the gallop and cantered, in an orderly crocodile, up to the trainer standing at the top of the long grass stretch. We circled round him awaiting the next item on the programme, during which the horses would go off in twos and threes to gallop back up the line of hurdles. To my surprise—for I was not normally allowed to school juveniles—I was told to mount the little black four-year-old which had jiggled about so enthusiastically at the back of the string. We trotted off to accompany an older horse up the line of hurdles. My mount had a rather skinny neck sticking up out of a pair of narrow shoulders. A pair of excited black ears, enthusiastically pricked, almost tickled my nose as we trotted off. He seemed a gay, honest and cheerful little horse, but no more.

When we turned to gallop back over the hurdles, however. I suddenly realised that this little piece of black wire possessed exceptional quality. He was obviously thrilled to see the first flight of hurdles and, instead of hesitating as most young horses do on such occasions, he increased his speed. With a quick, confident adjustment of his stride he sailed over the hurdle, gaining a full length on his more experienced partner, and then treated the remaining obstacles in the same way. I was thrilled. I had never ridden a youngster which felt like this. We went back and did it again, and this time I admired even more his quick, flashing stride and the care which he took to avoid touching the hurdles. By the time I got off I had fallen in love with him.

"Two thousand pounds," said Alec sadly, for he knew how much I wanted the horse. I gaped. It seemed an absurd price for an unimpressive-looking little horse which had never even seen a race-course. "No," said Alec, "they think a lot of him in Ireland and he's got the reputation of an exceptional jumper—that's the price I'm afraid." And so the matter rested, for the time being.

In the event he proved cheap at two thousand, for within a couple of months Workboy had won his first steeplechase. As a four-year-old he won two races and by the time he was six was rated possibly the best two-mile steeplechaser in the country. His skinny frame filled out, he grew, and with his gleaming black coat he developed into an impressive personality, far removed from my funny little friend of August, 1949.

Workboy had a very hard racing career. He was full of courage and will to win, and he very rarely had an off day. Consequently he was a good horse on which to bet, and ran frequently as a result. He was not built to carry heavy weights, and he was involved in many gruelling finishes. He became well known in the racing world for his courage and jumping, and beloved by the stablemen for his character and kindliness. As one of the stable amateurs I would see and covet him often, and many times I regretted that in some desperate fashion I had not raised that two thousand pounds.

In 1949 I made the acquaintance of another horse which was to be heard of again. He was not a very distinguished racehorse, though he had won one race, and he had strained a tendon badly in the previous season. His owner, a brother officer, asked me to ride the horse in a race at Wincanton and tell him what I thought of Fourtowns, as it was called. On my return I told him that the horse was not fast enough for racing but that when I jumped the first fence I had felt as if we were never coming down. "Make him into a showjumper," I said jokingly. My advice, not at all to my surprise, was not taken and the horse ran again with some-one else up, at Cheltenham, and with much the same result. A keen pair of eyes in the crowd had this time marked him down, and in a few days' time a young lady bore him away in her ancient horsebox—Pat Smythe had found Prince Hal.

The years passed. I became a pentathlete, went back to steeplechasing, Ronnie Cronin knocked me down and Pointsman momentarily picked me up. I painted and wrote occasional articles. Showjumping stayed in the background. One day, just as we were setting off for Yorkshire where I was to command my regiment, Harry Llewellyn asked me to ride his mare Lady Jane at the Horse of the Year Show at Harringay.

I can only imagine that Harry was casting about for likely showjumping recruits, for my efforts on Sarah six years earlier had long since faded into the mists. I had never ridden in a show of this magnitude, and standards had, in any case, risen considerably since I had last jumped seriously. I accepted—for to refuse would have been unthinkably faint-hearted—with grave misgivings.

This was the equivalent of being flung in at the deep end. I knew none of the showjumping personalities and the whole atmosphere of an international indoor show was strange to me. The fences looked huge and the space impossibly restricted. Lady Jane was, however, an old hand—too old in fact, for she was apt, in the vernacular, to drop a toe. This meant that she was not too particular about picking up her feet when confronted with an obstacle which did not impress her, but she knew her way round and needed little help from her rider. This was just as well. Our first round resulted in what is rudely known as a cricket score, but with Harry's help and advice our scoring rate was restricted gradually throughout the week. Indeed, we finished the show with two rosettes, of the mauve and pink variety associated with the lower awards, but none the less a far better outcome than I had expected.

As a result Harry Llewellyn lent me his veteran Olympic horse Monty to jump in 1955. This distinguished but now venerable figure—his age had passed beyond the point at which record could decently be kept of it—gave me the opportunity of appearing at a few shows, but he was really past serious jumping. We achieved a few minor successes together but as soon as the ground became hard his legs gave up the struggle. I enjoyed my showjumping, and learnt how much time, perseverance and luck—and how exceptional a horse—one would need to achieve international standing. I entertained no extravagant showjumping ambitions, for I could not see how I would ever be in a position to fulfil them.

One day that summer, quite casually, I picked up a copy

of *Horse and Hound* before lunch and in so doing altered the course of my life. I idly looked through its pages, not really noticing what was in them, when suddenly my eye fell on the catalogue for Ascot Sales. With a shock I saw that Workboy was on the list. In response to urgent calls, my wife came running; together we gazed at the notice: *Workboy, aged ten years, winner of thirteen steeplechases, including* . . . What the notice did not say, but what we knew, was that he had strained a tendon badly in the previous season, and was of doubtful soundness. To buy him now would be a gamble—but in any case was it possible to buy him, for the sale was taking place that day?But no, on further examination he was to be sold on the second day: tomorrow. So strong and affectionate were our memories of Workboy that we never hesitated in our decision to buy him. At the time it seemed that fate had taken a hand, and so indeed it proved.

A few telephone calls later he was ours, for one hundred and thirty-seven pounds. Shortly after he was with us. He bore his ten years lightly and the only blemish he had to show for his forty-six races was the damaged tendon. This indeed looked most unpromising. It was bowed, and warm and spongy to touch.

The question was: "What now?" No thoughts of showjumping him had yet entered our heads, and after discussion we decided that he was to be my wife's hunter next season. But would his bad leg stand hunting? We decided we had better find this out before the season began.

For the next two weeks he was schooled on the flat, and over small fences. He was like all racehorses, entirely ignorant of anything but the most elementary aids—he knew that when you pulled on the reins he ought to stop, and that when you kicked with your heels he ought to go on, but that was about all. He was very excitable and anxious to please. If other horses came into view, or more often if he became upset by a failure to understand what his rider wanted, he would work himself gradually into a state of frenzy, juddering and jiggling, flecked with foam and making no sense of any kind. He had a jerky uncomfortable trot, a high head carriage, and a stiff back. In fact, on the flat he was most unpromising material.

Over fences, however, it was a happier story. We began at once to school him over little showjumping obstacles, mainly to see if his tendon would stand up to work. We were at once delighted by the fluent way in which he dealt with them, and even more by his boldness and his care. Unlike most steeplechasers he understood how to jump wooden rails, much to our surprise, for we only discovered later that he had been carefully schooled in Ireland over natural obstacles, and indeed hunted, before he ever started to race. However, his bad leg got worse; cursing ourselves mildly for the light-hearted way in which we had acquired an elderly and unsound horse, we decided to fire his forelegs and rest him for six months.

The firing was done by Dr John Burkhardt and well done too, for never again did that tendon cause Workboy even one day's unsoundness. He emerged from his retirement in the middle of the hunting season, and gave my poor wife the most terrible day's hunting she has ever had. For once in a while the Zetland had no sport on that day, and Workboy, deprived of the gallop which he expected, nearly took leave of his senses. Horse and rider returned exhausted and worn, and only my wife's pleas to try again prevented me from putting him back into training as a racehorse. She tried him again and this time they had a good hunt. This settled him down considerably and they finished the season with growing confidence. Workboy was obviously a superb jumper, and as he had only had half a season's hunting we decided that he might as well pass the summer as my wife's showjumper. Regimental life was busy that spring and it was not until June that Workboy received much showjumping education. He was thus eleven years old before he was introduced to the sport, and as a distinguished ex-steeplechaser had one career behind him already.

We erected some home-made and rudimentary show-jumping fences in the paddock behind our house. We made use of several oil drums, and a spare door painted red did duty as a wall. Various branches were cut from trees and painted white. Improvisation and hope were our watch-words.

To train a horse you try to understand its personality and the way its mind works. All are different and, as in human beings, the more intelligence and character a horse has, the more imagination and tact are required to know it well. In some ways it is easier to train a young un-sophisticated horse with no experience of jumping, and which has acquired no habits, good or bad, than a hardened campaigner. Although the young horse will lack confidence and be more easily alarmed, at least you can mould it from the start. Against this possible disadvantage nothing quickens horses' reactions so much as steeplechasing or hurdling; they are constantly having to make split-second decisions to avert disaster and in consequence their brains learn to work far more quickly than normal.

A top-class two-mile steeplechase is the fastest form of jumping over big obstacles. The habits of six seasons' steeplechasing against the fastest horses in the land can never really be eradicated. At least so, rightly or wrongly, we decided shortly after we had begun to train Workboy over showjumps. At first we schooled him over obstacles at a trot in the approved fashion, widening them gradually and making him use his jumping muscles to the full. But we soon discovered that this did not suit him at all; the transition from jumping at a very fast gallop to trotting over fences was too sharp. To trot right underneath a couple of poles and then heave himself over them was a procedure which to him bore no relationship at all to the quick swoop and flat trajectory of steeplechase jumping. Sometimes, in desperation, he would take off a stride too soon and hurl himself unhappily into the middle of the obstacle. He was so bold and willing that despite the crashing of poles and uncomfortable bumping of legs that would ensue, he would always try again, and would next time launch himself into an even bigger bound, usually with the same result. The jumps he made over these small obstacles were prodigious but frequently misdirected, and it was obvious that if we continued like this we would wreck even nerves as good as his. In the accepted method of jumping training he was a fish out of water, and likely to remain so.

It may be that we should have lowered the obstacles almost to the ground and continued, day after day, trotting him over them as we raised and widened them. But, even if we had wanted to, we would never have had the time. Poor Workboy surmounted many obstacles in his show-jumping career, and the biggest was one called "not enough time". I never had enough time to train and prepare him as I should have done, and so often his own brilliance and initiative had to act as substitutes. At all events, on this occasion we decided to abandon the trotting technique, and henceforth we cantered him over fences as slowly as he would allow us to take him. He had a good mouth but a fiery and impetuous nature which racing had done nothing to improve, and even the new path was not always a very smooth one.

He still much preferred taking off a full stride or two earlier than was necessary. His spring, and indeed his style, were like a stag's, and capable of carrying him over most of our obstacles however far in front of them he took off, but these were small fences. He would not be able to do this over big ones, particularly wide spreads. Indeed, in his first season the fence which caused him most trouble was the triple bar, usually considered the easiest fence in the course. Unless he met this fence right in stride he would tend to launch himself into space far too soon and land in the middle.

We stumbled on with his training, making mistakes and retracing our steps when necessary, but all the time encouraged by his wonderful natural ability, his care, and desire to please. It was a long time before we discovered how best to ride him, and it was not until his second season that we began to get the technique right. Until then we had tried to make him jump his round carefully and deliberately, and we were, I suppose, slow in the uptake not to have realised earlier that the faster you could safely take him, and the more like a steeplechase you could make his round, the more confidently he would go.

Another great trial to a horse used to galloping on spacious race-tracks is the double fence and combination obstacle. Its natural reaction when advancing upon a fence with another fence only a stride beyond it is one of horror. Accustomed to landing far beyond its jumps on the racecourse, it estimates that it will probably land over the first fence into the roots of the second, which will then trip it up. The distances between showjumps in a combination are, of course, calculated at showjumping speed and not racing speed, so this disaster is in fact unlikely to befall it, but the underlying apprehension is at first always there. Moreover, the mere necessity of landing only to take off again is novel and alarming, particularly to the racehorse. In my experience, far more trouble and loss of confidence are caused by the combination fence than any other, and it is folly to ask a novice showjumper to make an appearance in public until it is jumping such fences confidently at home.

I had intended that Workboy should open his new career in one of the new Foxhunter competitions, over the least exacting course I could find, but at that time it was almost impossible to locate one in the conservative north. In the end, Workboy had to make his *début* over a more impressive course than I had intended. When my wife and he completed it with only one refusal and one knockdown we were surprised and relieved. Only a really bold horse with talent could have negotiated such a course so well on its first appearance.

On the next occasion he was third in a novice class, and then put up a magnificent performance in the Grade C Championship of the North. He jumped one of the only two clear rounds, and was the runner-up. Afterwards we had to fend off the professionals who approached with fancy offers; Workboy, in the showjumping sphere, had arrived. My wife then, very typically, handed him over to me. I had had more experience, she said, and would do the horse more justice; she was determined not to ride him again. This was a real sacrifice, and Workboy's later successes were due in no small part to all the tact, sympathy and understanding which she had lavished on this far from easy horse during his early training.

And so my partnership with Workboy began, in August, 1956. We had our first win at the Durham County Show in the Grade C (novice) competition, and then, jumping for the first time in floodlights, won the similar competition, after five clear rounds, at the Belle Vue Stadium at Manchester. I then got ideas above my station and rode him in a big open competition against top-class horses; this was not a success and put me firmly back in my place. Workboy and I had been successful in the restricted circles in which we moved, but this episode made me see the facts of showjumping life with greater realism. Between us and the leading jumpers a great gulf was still fixed. I watched that autumn a film of the Olympic jumping at Stockholm, and saw Nizefela, Flanagan and Scorchin win their Bronze Medals over a course more imposing than anything of which I had dreamed. To me, the top stars remained figures on a television screen, polished and calm under the White City or Harringay floodlights; they lived in a different world, far removed from my tumbledown jumps and the door masquerading as a wall. But ambition was astir. I now realised that fate had presented me with the horse of a lifetime. He was good enough to jump that gulf, and I hoped I was too.

During the winter my regiment moved to Germany, and Workboy's second season was passed on the German circuit. This was most valuable training for us both in the stage of development which we had reached. In England I would soon, too soon, have won too much to continue in novice classes, and would from then on have had to jump Workboy in nothing but big open classes and over big courses. In Germany the gulf can be bridged painlessly by jumping in their Category M, in which, although open horses can compete, the fences are never more than four feet six inches high. The jump-off, and sometimes the first round, are decided against the clock; if you are ready for the bigger fences you jump in Category S in which time matters less.

The Germans are apt to run their shows in one area at a time, so that the top stars can all come. There is no way of dodging some of the experts as you often can in England, and we had to take on all comers. Thus almost at once we were jumping against Olympic stars like Winkler and Thiedemann. Although these continued to twinkle undisturbed above our heads, it was extremely educational to compete against them. At least I was no longer watching them on the television screen, and was actually in personal contact with them in competition. Now and again we won rosettes, and all the time we learned. So well built and laid out were the German courses, even at the small shows, that never once did I frighten Workboy and his confidence bounded.

By the end of the season we were jumping big courses, and beginning to hold our own with all but the very brightest stars. Workboy had jumped magnificently in the Hamburg Spring Derby (an occasion no longer unique for it has now been emulated at Hickstead), and although just out of the awards he had gone round this very formidable course with the same number of faults as the Olympic gold medallist, Winkler on Hella. This was not, I felt, too bad for a horse which in England would still have been graded a novice, and so ineligible to jump at the White City!

By the end of the season we had won enough money to put this right, and henceforth Workboy would be graded A in British shows. Since his *début* in June, 1956, it had taken him only sixteen shows to achieve the necessary two hundred pounds in winnings, which is exceptionally few by any standards and in particular since I was having to learn at the same time. As a reasonably conscientious commanding officer I had to limit Workboy's opportunities to conform to the intense training tempo of the Rhine Army.

In 1958 I finished my time in command, and was appointed Military Assistant to the Chief of the Imperial General Staff, the Army's head soldier. Field Marshal Sir Gerald Templer worked in the War Office in Whitehall, and next to his office was mine, containing twelve highly-coloured telephones, three junior Staff Officers, and trays piled high with papers, most of them highly secret.

For some months it was as much as I could do to acclimatise myself to these high military altitudes. I had to arrange the Field Marshal's programmes for him, regulate and filter the vast flow of papers addressed to him, prepare letters and material for speeches and generally organise his day. It was a world quite strange to me and for a while I was unable to relax; half my mind would be battling through the correspondence and minutes and the other half poised to deal with the unexpected. One of the telephones would ring, the caller would announce himself as a string of unknown initials and would have to be identified and dealt with; a high General would pop his head round the door and as he would be in plain clothes it was all too easy to fail to recognise him and treat him with suitable deference. Several times a day my buzzer buzzed and turned yellow, demanding my presence in the inner office. There my kind but undeniably formidable master would require me to do something for him or to tell him the answer to something else; if it were the latter I was usually unable to oblige him and would go scurrying off to get the necessary information. After a few weeks of this my mind and reactions were as agile and well-schooled as an international polo pony.

I worked a long day but an absorbingly interesting one, and I enjoyed the lack of routine. Every day was different, there was always some new drama, international, political or military, which affected us to a greater or lesser degree and often stood our day's programme on its head. Twice in that year I went on tour with the Field Marshal, to Africa and to Italy. We were fortunate to escape from Whitehall even for these brief interludes, for 1958 was internationally an unsettled year.

One day in July news of the revolution in Iraq broke unexpectedly upon Whitehall, and threw it into the greatest turmoil. A spate of political and military decisions, in which the CIGS was heavily involved, poured down upon us. The tempo in my office rose considerably. This was unfortunate for besides revolutions I had the White City International Horse Show to think about.

My showjumping season had, like the international situation, been unsettled. Workboy and I had jumped at the occasional weekend show with reasonable success, but he had by no means had a satisfactory preparation for the White City. In the Army, however, you tend to lead a hand-to-mouth existence, and must snatch opportunities when they occur. I was determined to ride at the White City; the chance might never come again. Now the Middle East had conspired to frustrate me.

Fortunately I had a most efficient assistant in Dick Jefferies, and while he nobly held the fort I made a series of rapid dashes to Shepherds Bush. However late I was due to jump at the White City I would have to return to the office afterwards and catch up with events, which were galloping much faster than any horse at the show. It was, however, well worth while. Surprisingly enough, I felt much fresher mentally on my return each evening than I had done when I left the office earlier in the day, despite the stress of competition and the battle against time and traffic.

We had a great deal more success at the White City than I expected, and were placed three times. Workboy appreciated the big, well-made obstacles and showed this with a clear round in his first competition there. I was not ambitious during the week and when we just missed qualifying for the *Daily Mail* Cup, the Championship of the show, I was not altogether sorry. Workboy's ability and spring, it was more than ever obvious, were good enough to take him into the top class, but he needed more schooling on the flat and more experience in big shows, particularly over combination obstacles. I took him to a few Saturday shows in August and found that his experience at the White City had greatly improved his confidence and knowledge.

During my leave in the late summer, we went to Brighton Show, where most of the showjumping fraternity were assembled. Here were good, big courses and tough opposition. Throughout the week Workboy jumped superbly but unluckily, and on the Saturday the tide turned. In the Championship of the South, against nearly all the top British horses and riders, we were third.

Now, I felt, caution could at last be laid aside. On my return from leave I spread before me, amongst the coloured telephones and the secret documents on my desk, the entry form for the Horse of the Year Show. I wrote the name Workboy against all the big competitions I could find there.

I filled in the intervening weeks, which were particularly busy ones, with early morning schooling sessions in the indoor riding school at Knightsbridge Barracks. My experience with Lady Jane had taught me how necessary, in a restricted indoor ring, it is to have your horse well schooled on the flat. The corners indoors are sharp, and often you find yourself advancing on a very large fence with a run of only a few strides; thus your horse must be handy and obedient if any success at all is to be hoped for.

Fortune smiled on me during the 1958 Horse of the Year Show. No international crises hampered my plans, and Workboy and I were both relaxed and confident in each other. He was in his element at Harringay. He loved crowds and the opportunity to show off. The ring was small for his galloping stride but the fences stood out clearly in the floodlight and he was determined not to hit them. In the Beaufort Stakes on the first day he won his section with a clear round and in the final was fifth. He was going brilliantly and I felt much encouraged.

On the next night was the Puissance, or Test. I had never before subjected him to this severe competition, in which six to eight large jumps are placed in the ring, the number being reduced after each round and the remainder heightened. The contest usually ends with two very large obstacles which are raised until the winner is found.

In the first round Workboy jumped easily and clear, with eleven others. Round he went again: clear; and again. Now there were six competitors left, to jump a wall at five feet nine and a rail at six feet three. Alan Oliver on Red Admiral was round clear, and so was Walmsley on Nugget. Workboy met the wall slightly wrong; I tried to put him right and succeeded in making matters worse; even then a brick only just rolled out. Round the ring he galloped and sailed magnificently over the six feet three rail. We were third.

We reached the final of the Leading Jumper of the Year competition, having won our section and completed an exciting week by coming third in the *Sunday Graphic* Cup on the last night, the Championship of the Show. Workboy and I had jumped the gulf across which we had looked so hopefully two seasons before.

Thanks to the courage and ability of this old black horse, with one honourable career behind him, and acquired through a stroke of purest chance, a new world opened before us. We were selected to train for future international teams, and to be given as much overseas experience as possible. I was too pleased at the news to worry overmuch about the problems of combining all this with Whitehall. After all, I had lived a double life before.

CHAPTER TWELVE

South American Way

AFTER my Harringay excitement I settled back into the Whitehall roundabout. Except for a flying trip to Cyprus, the most troublesome of the problem children of the time, our winter was comparatively quiet. Workboy exercised peacefully in the Row, building up energy for Olympic training due to start in early April. It was the close season for showjumping, or so I thought.

One day I opened a letter from Colonel Mike Ansell, chairman of the British Show Jumping Association, inviting Pat Smythe and myself to go and jump for Great Britain in Chile. At first I was convinced that a year of Whitehall had at last unhinged me—an eventuality which was always on the cards—but after several deep breaths I assured myself that the letter was real, and read on. We were to compete in the Inter-Continental Show Jumping Championship to be held in February in Viña del Mar—in the stadium, in fact, where a semi-final of the World Football Cup was played in 1962.

The idea behind this event was a new one in showjumping circles. Each of the main showjumping nations had been invited to send two riders to compete, and the invitation had been accepted by Great Britain, France, Italy, Germany, Spain, the Argentine, Colombia and Chile. There would thus be sixteen riders, and they would all ride South American horses provided on the spot. Immediately before the Championship the Inter-American Horse Show would be taking place in Chile and nearly every horse worth considering in South America was to compete there. The sixteen most successful horses at this Show were to be pooled and drawn for, and the Championship was to go to the rider with the fewest faults at the end of a week's jumping.

The new CIGS, General Sir Francis Festing, was, as can be imagined, mildly surprised when I asked him if I could go to South America at short notice, but he kindly raised no objection. Whitehall was quiet, the annual February convulsion over the Defence White Paper had just subsided, and provided I was back a few days before the CIGS was due to waft me away to tour the Middle East and Africa in March, my way was clear. I found it very hard to take in that in a few days' time I was to fly out of the ice and fog of grey February London, to a country almost as far away as it was possible to go, to hot sun and high summer. My fellow workers in Whitehall found it even harder to comprehend what I was up to. When I explained to them that what they proposed for me next week was not practicable because I would be in Chile, they looked mildly disbelieving and passed on to something else. One day, however, I really did go to Chile, and then they had to believe me.

Lisbon, milder than London but still wintry, was the last contact with Europe. Then there was a long, long night over the Atlantic before, bleary-eyed, we touched down at Recife. Brazil—hot, steamy air which made our London winter clothes insupportable, palm trees, an air of indolent languor, smells, and canned South American music over the airport loudspeakers. Several orange squashes later we took off for Rio de Janeiro, flying for much of the way along the east coast of South America. I sat gazing fascinated down as the endless sandy, palm tree-studded landscape unrolled below, vast and almost unin-

Madrid 1960. Left to right: D. Bunn, Dawn Wofford, a Spanish liaison officer, Jack Talbot-Ponsonby, M. Charlesworth, Ann Townsend and the Author.

(Right) Jumping in the 1960 Imperial Cup at the White City.

(Below) The British team in Rome, 1961.

The Rome International Horse Show, 1961.

habited. Silly South American songs of my youth kept trickling into my head and tinkling round it in catchy rhythm. As I caught sight of Rio, with its enormous statue of Christ looking down from the hills to the sweep of its bay, to Copacobana beach, I was "rolling down to Rio" as Fred Astaire and Ginger Rogers once did. Over Buenos Aires I was subconsciously wriggling my hips with Betty Grable "down Argentina way". The magnificent brown grandeur of the Andes—a tremendous vista as you fly over them—only brought out a ridiculous jingle from a pre-war cabaret turn—Jack and Daphne Barker singing something which ended "from the Indies to the Andes in a scanty pair of panties is a very very daring thing to do". I wasn't feeling very daring when I landed in Santiago that evening, merely rather sleepy, sated with scenery and bemused by thirty-six hours of buzzing aero engines. When I sat down to dinner that night it was in fact seven o'clock in the morning in London so it was perhaps understandable that I found conversation an effort.

My team mate, Pat Smythe, had met me and led me off to stay with the Valdes, kind friends of hers and soon to be friends of mine. I could not have had a more entertaining partner. Pat loves going abroad but perhaps her favourite destinations are Spain and Latin America. She has used her talent for showjumping as a springboard and not, in the words of a famous man, as a sofa. She does not lie back, dreaming only of coloured poles and horses jumping them, she springs upon any country she visits and extracts as much fun from and information about it as she can; at the same time making many friends. She has taught herself Spanish and at least three other languages besides, she is liable to burst at almost any moment into Spanish American song accompanied by her guitar, and in her few spare moments, inexhaustible, she picks up her pen and writes a bit more of her latest book.

Chile, as most people know, is a remarkable shape, being about two thousand miles long and a hundred miles wide.

F

The north is desert where it rarely—if ever—rains; in the south you are on the way to Antarctica. In the centre, as in Santiago and Valparaiso, with the holiday resort of Viña del Mar, a cold sea current comes up the coast and converts the climate into one not unlike that of Kenya, hot but not insupportably so by day, and cool at night. From Santiago you can motor up to the Andes fifty miles away to superb ski-ing; fifty miles in the other direction you are on the Pacific Ocean. For all the pretensions of Santiago it is a backward country; for all the people's charm there is a honky-tonk air about even the most fashionable streets, and little worth buying in the shops. Its fascination lies in its inaccessibility, its strangeness, its beauty and its friendliness. The people are delightful; they refuse to take life seriously and have an altogether sensible lack of concern for time. *Mañana* (tomorrow) is their motto and it is infectious; after a week my tread was noticeably less brisk and my Whitehall punctuality dropped from me.

Having heard, before we left England, that European support for this enterprise was dubious, we were surprised at the constellation that had in fact assembled. Germany had sent Hans Winkler, the then Olympic champion, saturnine, correct and uneasily conscious of his crown. With him was his wife Inge, a good but not exceptional horsewoman, pleasant and cheerful but overshadowed by the great man. Piero d'Inzeo, with his solemn clown's face and his classic seat, represented Italy—brother Raimondo fell out at the last moment, reducing our number to fifteen and depriving us of the simultaneous presence of the reigning Olympic gold, silver and bronze medallists.

Spain sent two cheerful and efficient performers in Paco Goyoaga, a former World Champion, and Commandante Espinosa de los Monteros, possessor of a memorable clanking French accent and eleven children. From France came Capitaine de Fombelle, a prickly and determined character, permanently smouldering; he took against South America from the first day and from then on everything, in his view, was expressly arranged to annoy him. Pierre d'Oriolà, his team mate and former Olympic gold medallist, was very different: calm, aristocratic, possessed of great charm and, on a horse, of a style more truly classic than any of the celebrated riders present. He is, however, a great man for a party, and he and Paco Goyoaga rarely if ever got home before breakfast; they stoutly maintained that they jumped much better that way and presumably they should know. To all these varied Europeans were added the best two riders from the Argentine, Chile and Colombia.

There was not much horse show business for the first few days, and we were able to enjoy the hospitality of friends and to bask in the sun. Bathing in the Pacific off Chile is wonderful—cold, but the sun soon warms you and the rollers are magnificent. I soon learnt to treat these rollers with respect after I received a direct hit from one when my attention was elsewhere; it felt like being hit by a bus and I was lucky not to get hurt. I thought of the reception I should receive from Colonel Ansell and his committee (or without his committee for that matter) if I had to explain to them that after being sent to Chile at vast expense I had been incapacitated by a wave. The thought was sobering, and I became more careful.

In the evenings we would go to the Inter-American Horse Show to get a preview of our possible mounts. They were all competing there, and the sixteen with the most points would be reserved for us on the following week. I think we all got a pretty good idea of the horses we would like to have, and vice versa. On the whole they were fairly level—the most successful was an Argentine horse called S'il vous plaît which was obviously rather awkward to ride, and there were several others I liked as much or more. In particular I fancied a big chestnut Argentine called Stromboli, rather excitable but intelligent and with a great spring. At the ringside we amused ourselves by sticking pins into the list of possibles and my pin got Stromboli. But that seemed unlucky—I couldn't surely get him twice.

The conference at which the teams were briefed was much like any international conference—it went on for hours; everyone talked but nobody listened. A knowledge of Spanish, which neither I nor several others possessed, would have been a great help, and I had to rely on de los Monteros translating some of it to me in his extraordinary French, while I passed it on to the Winklers in English. There was a good deal of contention and nothing was really changed during the discussion, but the real purpose of the conference, which was to allow everyone to blow off steam, was amply fulfilled.

At the end of it, the position was that having drawn our horse we would ride it in three competitions, the first a speed contest over smallish fences, the next a Puissance over a few big fences, and the last a Nations' Cup course of two rounds over a long course of big fences. The four riders with the most points would classify for the final, to be ridden on the fourth and last evening. This final would be run on what used to be European Championship lines: each rider would first complete the course on his own horse and then ride three more rounds, changing horses with his opponents after each round. The rider with the fewest faults would be acclaimed Champion.

But first we had to make the all-important *sorteo,* the draw. This was conducted before a large gathering and with much ceremony; and it began with what promised to develop into a first-class row between the Europeans and the South Americans. It revolved round the heads of the three South American riders whose own horses were numbered among the sixteen. What, it was asked, would happen should one of them draw his own horse? The Europeans maintained that he should put it back and try again; the South Americans objected. The Chairman handled it very well; he sat impassively until no one could think of anything more to say and then announced that there was nothing in the rules to prevent anyone riding his own horse, that our Federations had had the schedule

and had not objected, and that was that. After a few re-
bellious mutterings the Europeans subsided, and the draw
began.

The inevitable at once occurred. Arrambide of the
Argentine was first to draw; he put in his hand and in a
slightly embarrassed voice read out the name of S'il vous
plaît, not only his own horse but the Number One of the
sixteen selected. I am glad to say that even the Europeans
roared with laughter, and the draw continued. There was
one horse which everyone hoped to avoid; a large ponder-
ous animal called Huaso whose selection was something of
a mystery. As each of us walked up to draw he was followed
by derisive shouts of "Huaso" from the rest; Paco Goyoaga
had shouted with more enthusiasm than any, and when he
unfolded his piece of paper and read the fateful name he
temporarily lost his ability to see the funny side. It was
indeed bad luck, as he never had a chance from that
moment onwards. Huaso was thoroughly unpredictable;
at one moment clambering over obstacles and splintering
them to matchwood and at the next doing a splendid clear
round. Anyway it was a relief to get Huaso out of the way,
but when I opened my paper and read out the word Stromboli I knew it really was my lucky day. I had no excuses
now. Pat drew a Chilean horse called Simbad which had
pretty good form. Winkler had drawn the Number Two
horse which was reputed to be good but difficult, d'Inzeo a
Chilean Olympic horse, de los Monteros a very good
Colombian horse, d'Oriolà a good Argentine; in fact no
one except the unfortunate Goyoaga had any cause for
complaint. Besides Arrambide a Chilean called Zuniga had
drawn his own horse, a good old warrior called Pillan.

The next step was to try the horses—a very formal and
highly organised function, attended by all the owners and
quite a few of the general public. We were allowed an
hour on two mornings, during which hour we could jump
six fences. This condition was carefully controlled and if by
any chance a competitor miscounted and jumped seven he

was to be eliminated from the whole competition. Nobody did. These periods were eventful. De los Monteros emerged from one with a heavily plastered chin and the owners, who not unnaturally were watching their horses lynx-like from the stand, kept bounding forward to offer criticism and advice. This help was not always welcomed, and coolness developed between certain riders and their owners; indeed de Fombelle and his owner ended the two sessions barely on speaking terms.

Luckily the British sessions were harmonious from every point of view. I could not have had more charming owners than Pedro and Elena Majorga, and indeed Elena was so glamorous that it was quite difficult to concentrate on my riding. Stromboli was excitable, but so was Workboy and I was used to that; otherwise he was not difficult to ride and was beautifully schooled. Pat was not so sure of hers. It was a smallish thoroughbred with a great spring but an awkward head carriage. However, it went very well for her, and the owner was delighted.

At long last the preliminaries, the receptions, the handshaking, the welcomes were all over, and there was nothing for it but to go into the ring and do the best we could. Every night the show started at ten o'clock which meant that it was unusual to get to bed before three even if we went straight back to the hotel, which seldom happened. At least it was cool then—in fact, you needed an overcoat. The arena was vast, and was well filled. The crowd was capable of a tremendous yell and was no respecter of persons. It started as it meant to go on by giving Prince Bernhard, who had come over to preside at the show, a cheerfully hostile reception. He was reputed to have made some uncomplimentary remarks about Chile after a previous visit; judging from the storm of whistling which greeted him he was not getting the benefit of the doubt. He took it all quite happily.

The show began with the usual parade. We all rode in behind our flags borne by Chilean equestriennes; the

Union Jack, inevitably, was upside down. Some of the national anthems were very long (the Argentine one is interminable), and after half an hour at the salute Piero d'Inzeo and I had just agreed to start saluting with our left hands when the ordeal mercifully ended. But no, it was not ended, the speeches of welcome began. The crowd soon got bored with this and a further bout of whistling ensued. Shortly afterwards we started.

The first competition, as already mentioned, was against the clock, over a reasonably small course. You could jump two practice fences in the corner before beginning your round, and some riders, particularly Winkler, brought their horses into these out of stride so as to give their legs a warning clout. Winkler went round slowly, with one fence down. Pat was next in and at once caused a stir by being flung violently on to one of the practice jumps by a sharp refusal. She broke her reins and there was nothing for it but to run into the ring and help. The Chilean crowd had never seen my uniform before, blue with green and primrose breeches and cap, chain mail on shoulders and gold crossbelt, and were momentarily stunned when this vision ran into the ring. Not for long, though, and I was greeted with wild hoots, whistles and shrieks of derision. In this tumult I helped Pat fix her reins and ran thankfully back into obscurity. Pat's blood by now was up and she chased Simbad round the course for a brilliant performance, the fastest round of the evening and only marred by an unlucky foot in the water. It was not until d'Inzeo came in and did a steady clear that she was beaten.

Stromboli eventually entered in a high state of excitement, calming down when he began. I made the silly error of trying to be too ambitious and win it with a fast clear. This was very stupid for Stromboli was not a speed merchant, and it would have been much better to have tried for a slow clear—which would as it turned out have put me second. As it was I raced round asking him to reach for his fences as if I had been riding Workboy. It was a bad round; I had three down and although the Majorgas and Pat were kind afterwards I wished that Pacific wave had sucked me out to a watery grave. It was obvious that I must ride Stromboli much more deliberately, accurately and calmly.

I approached the next night's performance, the Puissance, with a distinct needle. This was my first international appearance, and so far I had not been a success. I could not afford another nonsense. There were eight fences, fairly big but well presented, and the course did not look difficult. Nor was it, for out of fifteen horses, eleven went clear. Of these mercifully Stromboli was one. It was one of the most important rounds I ever jumped; one fence down would have put me right out of the running in the Championship and would have shaken my confidence in the international sphere. But I never had a moment's worry as soon as we had started. Between fences I was now hooking him right back till he was balanced and placed, and then letting him surge smoothly forward at the jump. His great spring, his conscientiousness and intelligence did all the rest. I returned to base with a great load off my mind.

The fences were raised for the jump-off, and as only one barrage is allowed in an international Puissance they went pretty high. Again Stromboli sailed round for a clear. So did Arrambide with S'il vous plaît, d'Oriolà, the Chilean with Pillan, and by some miracle—Huaso! Winkler had eight faults and d'Inzeo four. Pat had a stop at a very big spread and I got the uncomfortable impression that Simbad was beginning to see the red light. But at the end she lay equal third in the overall placings with d'Inzeo, with the two South Americans who had drawn their own horses leading the field. I had gone up to seventh and all was not yet lost.

The Nations' Cup course on the third night was big, and long. It was to be ridden twice. It was a Saturday night, and the event had obviously caught on, for the crowd was vast. I came in early, to one of the most enjoyable rides of my life, for Stromboli just sailed round. We met everything plumb right and he never looked like making a fault—we got a great reception. There was a good deal more incident in this competition, and various rather shaky partnerships came unstuck. Even Winkler, who had not by any means hit it off with his horse, had twelve faults, d'Inzeo had four, and none of the South Americans was clear. De los Monteros joined me with a clear, and then d'Oriolà.

My forebodings about Simbad were justified. He stopped again at one of the practice jumps, and then performed as if his nerve were rapidly leaving him. I can't think who else but Pat would have got him round this formidable course with only eight faults. I was dreading her second round, and sure enough at the second fence he stopped very quickly and gave her a nasty fall. She was shaken up and hurt, but rose to her feet, remounted, forced him over the obstacle by sheer will-power and then achieved the near-miracle of getting him round the rest of the course clear. The crowd went quite mad. They rose to her and cheered for a full minute. And rightly so, for it was the most brilliant display of courage and riding skill that I have ever seen in my life. As I remarked at the time, she could not have done more for British prestige in South America if she had won all the competitions and been accompanied by ten trade delegations. But, of course, as far as qualification for the final was concerned the fall and the time faults had put her right out of it.

My second round on Stromboli was not quite so good as the first. He had got very stirred up and was more difficult to steady; perhaps in addition I may have been over-cautious. Anyway we had one down. D'Oriolà, one of the other first round clears, this time had twelve faults, but de los Monteros went clear again, to win it. I was second, and this qualified me for the final of the Championship, with a lead of half a point over the unlucky de los

Monteros. The other qualifiers were the two South Americans on their own horses, and d'Oriolà. An unexpected fall by the wayside was that of Piero d'Inzeo, whose second round collected no fewer than twenty faults. It was difficult to see what was going wrong; he appeared to be as smooth as ever and the horse was a good one, but one by one the fences fell down. To be honest I was not sorry to see him out of the final. Without making odious comparisons I joyfully settled for the two South Americans in preference to either d'Inzeo or Winkler. One gold medallist (d'Oriolà) was quite enough to compete with, let alone two and a bronze.

Before the final there was a rest day, and Pat and I drove off into the country to see a rodeo. The other competitors were supposed to accompany us but for various reasons did not come under starter's orders—Paco Goyoaga and d'Oriolà, for example, because they had only just gone to bed when we were due to leave. The further we got from the Pacific the hotter it became, and when we reached the rodeo it was baking. We were received with much ceremony by the *huasos,* the Chilean cowboys, and went up into the stand to watch the proceedings. These consisted of a small bullock being chased back and forth round the ring by a couple of hefty *huasos*; the idea being to turn it between two marks on the walls by bashing it with the horses against the wooden wall so that it spun round and set off in the opposite direction. It was a colourful and unusual spectacle but that was about all you could say for it; I admired the *huasos'* flat hats and gay ponchos, and the dash with which they rode, but felt rather sorry for the unfortunate bullocks. Now and again one lay down and refused to play; I had much sympathy with it. After a while it got altogether too hot to sit in the open stand and we withdrew to the shade for refreshment.

This was much better. We sat in what would be called a marquee in England, except that it had open sides and its roof consisted of thin reed thatching through which the sun cast attractive dappled shadows on the wooden floor. We drank a mauvy-grey drink which was pleasant and I should think fairly potent. A woman in national dress appeared with a guitar and sang to us; a small band materialised and she laid down her guitar, picked up some castanets and, with her husband, went into a seductive South American dance. The rhythm, the castanets and the drink, the floor mottled with sunshine and the gaiety, made Whitehall seem a long long distance away.

After this the party developed and *huasos* crowded in to join us. Soon we were dressing up in their hats and ponchos, and riding their horses about—gay, uninhibited people enjoying our fiesta. Much later in the cool of the evening we left for Viña del Mar, and, for me, the Championship final next day.

This took place at six o'clock in the evening in hot sunshine and again before a capacity crowd. It began with much photographing and Press activity, and then the four finalists came in, to be penned in a small corral at the end of the arena. We were to remain in this corral, unless performing, until the end. We were thus in the ring for nearly two hours. I became so absorbed in the competition that neither time nor the crowds' reactions registered with me at all, and it was not until I got up on my fourth horse that I realised I felt quite tired. I suppose the contest was a strain subconsciously, but I never felt it till afterwards.

I had worked out the problem beforehand, and it seemed to me that d'Oriolà's horse, Virrey, was likely to be the crucial one. D'Oriolà had a definite advantage in riding him first, for in previous contests the horse had tended to become idler as the competition wore on. I hoped very much that I would draw him second, or at least third. The Chilean, Zuniga's horse Pillan was a nice cosy old number; he was very experienced and had jumped in the Helsinki Olympics. He presented no problem. Arrambide's horse S'il vous plaît was reputedly difficult, but I had watched him carefully and was not too worried. Like many Argentines he would get worked up in the ring, and he had to be prevented from rushing his fences. His owner did this by advancing crabwise at each obstacle until he reckoned the moment had come to point the horse at it. It was just a question of switching him round at the right moment; otherwise the horse was brilliant. We made the draw, and Arrambide was to go first, myself second, Zuniga the Chilean third, and last d'Oriolà. This meant that I rode Pillan second, Virrey third and S'il vous plaît last. It could have been worse; I might have got Virrey last.

The course looked easy but in fact was not. There were two difficult fences, the third which was a tricky combination, and the sixth, a high and flimsy gate. The last fence, the water, had two poles over it and was very easy. Our impression was that all four horses with their regular riders on board would be sure to do a clear in the first round, but oddly enough not one did. We all had four faults; I made a muck of the combination with Stromboli, and the others all made some error.

We changed horses and each in turn had two minutes and two practice jumps before the next round. Arrambide led off with Stromboli and went round very luckily for four faults; he rattled one or two which did not fall. Pillan went well for me, but again I messed up the combination —four faults. Zuniga had an unhappy round on Virrey for twelve faults. D'Oriolà on S'il vous plaît made, I thought, a mistake. He rode him straight at every fence, unlike the owner, and with his lovely hands got away with it with only four faults, but he paid the penalty by going very slowly and incurring half a time fault. This half fault loomed very large later in the evening.

The third round started sensationally by Arrambide and Pillan crashing to earth through the combination and rolling on the ground. Neither was hurt but that alone cost Arrambide twelve faults. Zuniga did not compete very well with S'il vous plaît, and from now on the contest rested between myself and d'Oriolà.

I mounted Virrey knowing that this was my really important round. He was a calm and lazy Argentine, and over the practice jumps I suddenly discovered how to ride him. He reacted as do some German horses to firm, even rough, use of hands and legs. The technique was to yank him right back almost to a halt at the approach, then leg him on and finally as he took off give him the most fearful kick in the guts. To my delight he jumped round like a buck and never looked like touching anything, till we came to the last fence, the water. Here I was guilty of a fatal inexcusable lapse in concentration. I had been riding for all I was worth, and as I landed over the one-but-last fence I remember feeling a tremendous thrill of relief. We were as good as clear. Subconsciously I must have said to myself, "This fence is easy, nobody makes a fault here," only to find to my horror that I was coming into it dead out of stride. I pushed him frantically, but he couldn't do it, and just touched the tape. I have seldom felt so angry with myself, for I had a feeling that this was going to prove an expensive error. In fact it cost me the Championship.

D'Oriolà muttered his condolence as I passed. He looked a trifle strained, but at once rubbed salt into the wound riding my Stromboli round for a beautiful clear, the only one of the day. That meant that he led me by three and a half faults, with one round to go.

S'il vous plaît turned out as I had expected. He was a lovely horse and if you straightened him with even a very short run he had enough ability to jump most fences. I had bad luck with him at one fence; he was plumb right for it but must have dropped a foot, for the bar gently rolled off into the grass. Seven and a half faults behind d'Oriolà. He could afford one fence down, but not two, such was the baleful influence of his half fault for time.

Pillan was his mount. He was an easy old horse but had hit the earth very hard a short time before with Arrambide, and might be feeling sore now. D'Oriolà set off amid an expectant hush, broken only by the clatter of the third fence as it fell. He could not afford another. But, alas for our hopes, he did not need one, and with a tremendous yell the crowd greeted the winner of this unusual contest. He had won by three and a half faults, I was second, Arrambide third and Zuniga fourth. And so it all ended, amid the usual welter of photographers, Pressmen, congratulations, condolences and confusion. I bade old Stromboli an affectionate farewell and went off to get a drink.

I should like to have stayed longer in South America, which has unusual charm, and particularly because I could have gone with the other riders to jump in Mexico on the way home. But I had to lay aside my *Mañana* motto and make a dash for the next aircraft for England; if I missed it I would have also missed going with the CIGS to the Middle East and Africa. This would have been unpopular, and in any case I wanted very much to go with him.

It had been a wonderful three weeks, and soon, back in the March east wind, I was to wonder if it ever happened. It had been a good start to my time as an international showjumper and a great experience. But that final water jump still haunts me.

CHAPTER THIRTEEN

Workboy

By the time I had returned from South America, and from the subsequent military trip to Africa, the 1959 show-jumping season was upon us. Workboy, at the age of four-teen, was due to make his bow upon the international stage—indeed he was hustled on to it with very little preparation.

Our partnership was in its fourth season. During that time he had had no other rider, and I had competed on no other horse. I am, therefore, not the most experienced judge of how a top-class showjumper should feel to ride. Even so I cannot believe that he was the easiest of rides at this stage of his development. He was still very excitable, and preferred to jump his rounds at top speed as if he were still racing; indeed he jumped very much better that way. If he met a fence wrong his instinct still was to stand off it and reach, not to put in another stride and get close to it. Faced with some of the enormous spread fences which are put up now, or an impressive combination, he could not afford, indeed no horse other possibly than Sunsalve could afford, to take off several yards in front of it. Thus I as his rider, travelling at quite a fast gallop, had to time his stride into these big spreads and combinations; left to himself, disaster was probable.

Timing requires a good eye for a stride, in just the same

way as the good cricketer must have an eye for a ball. I possess quite a good natural eye, which improved with experience, but in 1959 it was not always equal to the occasion. I found too that one goes through periods when quite unaccountably one's eye is right out, and in the same way as cricketers go through a bad patch, so do show riders find themselves temporarily incapable of finding their stride. Pat Smythe is almost immune to this tiresome frailty, but very few others are. When my eye was out, Workboy and I were liable to find ourselves in trouble; when it was in, we would sail impeccably round big courses. Our reliability improved with the years.

Despite all his knocks and vicissitudes in two careers Workboy still loved jumping. From the age of three, when he was first taught, he always had. His intelligence and will-power had never impaired, as it does in some old horses of personality, his courage and his anxiety to please. He always did his best. His speed and his jumping power were, in combination, an unforgettable experience, and I always wished that his life had been long enough for three careers, so that I could have sailed round the cross-country course at Badminton on his back. Quite enough obstacles, however, lay ahead of us in the sphere we had chosen.

In 1959 the Rome Olympics were only a year away. The victorious team of Helsinki was scattered, Foxhunter and Aherlow dead, Nizefela in decline. Harry Llewellyn had retired, and such other good riders as remained on the scene were short of top-class horses. No single combination of horse and rider stood out as a certainty for the 1960 Olympics; the field was wide open.

Some ten or a dozen of the possibles were assembled in late March for training at Arundel. Facilities were generously lent by the Duke and Duchess of Norfolk in the park. I was a new boy on the international scene, and it was not for me to doubt the methods employed in this new venture of training a British team, or indeed the feasibility of training a team at all. It very soon became obvious to me, however, that as far as Workboy was concerned nothing but damage was being done. He, and I think probably his rider, were much better in competition than in practice. The jumping of big fences without the stimulus of battle, even though our chances of selection were involved, invited miscalculation and disaster. Within a week Workboy had taken a dislike to the whole arrangement, and shortly afterwards he had a sensational fall which to this day, I understand, is often watched with awe by the Arundel guests on the Duchess's cine projector. This fall nearly broke Workboy's neck, and, for a sensitive horse, must have shaken his nerve considerably. I took him home at once.

Such were the recuperative powers of his courage and physique that after ten days of the familiar, if haphazard, training methods at home he was back in his best form in time for Ascot Show. Our performance at Ascot, despite our unimpressive results in training, earned us a place in the team travelling to Lisbon and Madrid. I thus went abroad again, in this extraordinary year during which, though nominally located in Whitehall, I spent more than three months overseas on military and showjumping business.

I was now fully launched on this latest, and most intense, version of my double life. The soldiering side of it was obviously predominant, and I was fortunate in having a kind and understanding master in the CIGS, a very good assistant to do my work when I was away, and a summer free from international drama. Had 1959 been as active internationally as 1958 my programme would have been impossible; hence no one prayed more fervently or more selfishly than I did for peace in our time.

Even so, it was a split-second year. I went to Chile, was back in Whitehall for two days, and then accompanied the CIGS on a fortnight's tour of Africa. At odd moments I dashed down to Arundel to indulge in the process which I have laughingly described as training. Ascot Show—in-

cluding time off to see Pointsman run in the Whitbread
Gold Cup, and then Lisbon, Madrid, back in Whitehall
for three weeks, then the Barcelona Show. The climax of
the year was reached when I rode out of the ring at Barcelona at one o'clock in the morning, caught an aeroplane
to London at three, after breakfast rushed to the War
Office to collect some papers, met the CIGS at Northolt
and was watching him converse with Herr Willy Brandt
in Berlin before lunch. A Brigadier at the subsequent
lunch party, on being introduced to me, said, "Oh yes, are
you anything to do with the Blacker who rides in shows?"
It was strange to think not only that I was, but that I had
actually been riding in one twelve hours earlier, in Spain.

In Lisbon Workboy won his first international competition, and was third in the *Grand Prix*. In Madrid he
jumped superbly, and was a member of the British team
which won the Nations' Cup—another milestone in his
life. There was nothing very different in jumping abroad,
I found. The fences were basically the same, and there was
more accent on speed. The competition was if anything
often rather less severe than in the big English shows,
when all the professionals are there. It is the strangeness
of the atmosphere, the "foreignness" of it, which daunts
British riders until experience encourages them to relax
and show their home form in the ring.

Workboy returned from Spain a few days before the
White City International Horse Show. He was in brilliant
form throughout the week. On the second night he won
the Imperial Cup against the best the nations could bring.
For the past two seasons it had been won by foreign riders
since Nizefela and Wilf White captured it in 1956. We
beat Goyoaga of Spain by two-fifths of a second, and received the Cup from Mrs Mike Ansell, wife of my old
regimental friend and commander. Ten years before,
almost to the day, I had mounted a little black four-year-
old to do a gallop over hurdles; both of us absorbed with
racing and with never a thought for the White City spot-

light and the crowds standing to *God Save the Queen*.

If I had ridden more accurately and intelligently during the week, we would have won at least once more. Life in Whitehall was hectic at the time, and I suppose, to tell the truth, I was beginning to feel the strain. On the day following the Show I was to take off with the CIGS for a world tour. My mind was full of military preoccupations, and when you are taking on the best riders in the world you must be in a single-minded mood if you are to beat them. On form I had the best chance of any British rider that year to hold back the foreigners' grasp on the King George V Cup, and through careless riding had a pole down to put me out of it. In the *Daily Mail* Cup, the Championship of the Show, for which only the most successful twenty-four horses were eligible, I actually caught myself thinking of something quite different on three separate occasions during my round. You would hardly have thought this possible before thousands of people and the television cameras, but by then I was feeling very jaded indeed. Workboy was now able to look after himself, and despite my inattention he jumped miraculously round a difficult course to be one of seven horses clear, eventually finishing fourth. I hurried from the showground to board my aeroplane for Australia, feeling that, however indifferently I might have ridden him, Workboy at any rate had established himself in his first international season.

With six other riders and ten other horses, we were selected for the 1960 Olympic squad. The year began, as had the previous one, with training at Arundel. Remembering past experiences I did not at all wish to take part in this, but my selection depended on toeing the line and I dutifully and mistakenly disobeyed my instinct.

The story of the 1960 Olympic team is a painful one which, but for the fortuitous partnership of David Broome and Sunsalve at the eleventh hour, would have ended in total, instead of partial, failure. I have no wish to rake over dead wood, nor to conduct yet another of the post mortems so fashionable after the death of our hopes. The important result of the year's experiences has been an altogether different approach to the 1964 Olympics.

In 1960 the probable team was for much of the time insulated from the harsh, competitive world outside. English shows, it was felt, did not provide the right sort of courses over which to polish up an Olympic team; the probables competed at the White City and three shows abroad but otherwise remained aloof from the rough and tumble of the showjumping season. Now and again the team would proceed to a nearby English show and there, amid scenes of much pomp and ceremony, give an exhibition round a specially constructed Olympic-type course. This policy, good from some points of view, neither gave individual riders the chance to win their place in fair fight against all comers, nor enough competition. The present policy provides riders and horses, selected in the first place for their competitive ability, with the chance to prove themselves in world competition. It seems also to have been tacitly recognised that our top riders, unlike those of some other nations, do not respond ideally to centralised training. Our proved performers are individuals with their own ideas which are, I venture to think, too fixed to change. This, in the eyes of the purists, may be sad but is to a large extent true. The way to put the situation right is to look to the future, to catch prospective stars young, and train them on the correct lines in their teens. This is now being done.

For me, 1959 had been a year in which opportunity and good fortune had combined to form a memorable and unusual pattern. In 1960 I came down to earth again. Although I embarked on the Olympic training, I knew that I was—a fortnight later—to leave my job in London on promotion, and take over as Assistant Commandant at Sandhurst. A difficult clash of interests impended, but it never took place. Workboy solved my dilemma by responding so badly to his training sessions that it became obvious that we would have to withdraw. As I was about to take this bitter decision, it was taken for me; the team veterinary surgeon, in the course of a routine inspection, announced that Workboy's heart was in a condition which might make him dangerous to ride. This thunderbolt, for which I was unprepared, made my withdrawal in any case inevitable. A horse with a suspect heart has no place in an Olympic ring.

One of my first actions after installing Workboy at Sandhurst was to seek a second opinion on the state of his heart. It was sobering to realise, as the Olympic team vet had indicated, that I had been riding a horse which might drop dead at any moment, and it was only sensible to estimate what risks I was running in continuing to jump him. The second opinion was reassuring. Workboy's heart was certainly strained but provided it did not get worse, should not prove dangerously so. I continued therefore to jump him, checking his heart rate every three months. This never appeared to alter, and I gradually forgot about it.

We had a successful and lucrative summer at the English shows, and finished the season by winning the big prize at British Timken, against all the assembled home talent. At the White City Workboy was second in the Imperial Cup to Sue Cohen, who was in the all-conquering form which earned her four wins at the Show. I remember, best of all the competitions that summer, the King George V Cup.

This competition seldom fails to conjure up its own peculiar magic. The White City Stadium on lesser occasions can seem cold and impersonal even if it is almost full; when it is half empty it is sometimes cavernous and depressing. On the Wednesday night of the Show every seat is traditionally taken, every one of those acres of stone steps and serried enclosures is packed. The ring glows golden, shot with colour. Round it, towering back into the darkness and seeming all the vaster for being half concealed, the crowd mutters and hums with anticipation. Soon, as the competition begins, it will be seesawing in its excitement between cheers and groans, building up in intensity until a roof-raising yell hails the winner. In days long before I took up showjumping I had, on my occasional visits to the White City, been affected by the glamour and by the drama of this competition—this, I felt, was the one showjumping event in which I would give almost anything to compete.

At the 1960 White City, the American and the Argentine Olympic teams—the second of which included my old friend Stromboli—were the principal opponents for the British team and others such as myself. For several years now a foreigner had lifted the King George V Cup —in every year, in fact, since the heyday of Foxhunter. Workboy was at the top of his form, and we sailed round this big course clear, in company with ten others. The fences were raised, and the ten of us went again. One after another the horses made faults. Workboy rolled off a bar from a big combination which was set at just about his limit, for four faults. He had given everything of which he was possessed. Nobody had, however, gone clear; we were still in the running. With the last horse to go it looked as if another jump-off, for all those with four faults, impended. The last horse was Sunsalve, recently united with David Broome. Magnificently and impeccably this great combination swept round the big course like a galleon in full sail. With a resounding, rocking roar the crowd rose to these great, new-found saviours of British prestige—which had indeed risen that evening for amongst those equal second were Workboy and Peter Robeson on another rising star, Firecrest.

In 1960, despite Workboy's success at home, I felt on my departure from the Olympic team that as far as international events were concerned I was no longer one of the circle; I was an outsider looking in. In 1961 the pendulum suddenly swung dramatically back. Workboy and I were selected for the British team to visit Rome in May, and I was appointed team captain.

I did not receive much notice of this invitation, and it was not easy to get Workboy ready in time. A further complication was that I had decided to take a parachute course with the Sandhurst cadets, at Abingdon, and just before I was due to leave for Rome.

I had often wondered if parachuting was as terrifying as it looked from the ground. On a visit with the CIGS to the United States Airborne Forces I had talked to middle-aged and unathletic American Colonels who jumped regularly out of aeroplanes and thought nothing of it. As a middle-aged but still reasonably athletic British Brigadier I was determined not to lag behind; what they could do, I could do.

If it is possible to learn parachuting without tears you do so at Abingdon. The training, technically and psychologically, is beautifully executed by the admirable RAF instructors. I had, in any case, gone through the motions and expected sensations so often in imagination that when I actually jumped the experience came as no surprise to me. Even the first jump, from a barrage balloon, was not as bad as I expected, though a memorable occasion all the same.

Four of you clamber with the instructor into a small box-like compartment slung below the balloon. The balloon begins to rise rapidly. If you are brave enough to look down, the ground recedes alarmingly, and the ambulance waiting below grows smaller and smaller. Up you go. The instructor engages you in easy chat. You are glad that the parachute on your back is hooked firmly to a steel rod in the compartment; when you jump, the strap so attaching it will pull the parachute out automatically. You feel the handle of the reserve parachute on your chest and reassure yourself by thinking how exceptionally unlucky it would be if one after the other your two parachutes failed to open.

The balloon has stopped. From eight hundred feet up the ambulance looks like a toy. The compartment sways gently with the wind which moans quietly round the fuse-lage. Your fellow victims look thoughtful, your instructor brisk, as he checks your equipment and watches for the green smoke below which gives him the go-ahead. He turns to you. "Well, sir, stand in the door." This is it.

In the doorway, with one foot half over the edge above the void, you gaze tautly into space. Suddenly the expected hand descends on your shoulder; a voice shouts, "Go!" Automatically, eyes shut and giving yourself up for lost, you jump. Almost at once there is a reassuring crack above you and your descent is violently retarded. You open your eyes to look up at the parachute to see if it has opened properly, your hand clutching the reserve handle in case it has not. But there, swaying serenely above your head, is the most beautiful sight in the world at that moment, a perfectly opened canopy against the sky. Your apprehensions leave you; you know the drills and you carry them out. Below, a voice booms encouragingly at you through a megaphone. You descend peacefully. The view is lovely. There is plenty of time and nothing to worry about; you have mastered your drift and are fully in control. Suddenly the ground appears to rush madly up towards you and, long before you have decided on your landing position, there is a terrific thump and there you are lying, very surprised at still being alive, on *terra firma*.

The jumps from the balloon, silent, cold creature drooping cynically over that very small wooden compartment, are worse than those from the aircraft. No one, I believe, can ever treat a parachute descent of any kind lightheartedly. However often you jump it remains an un-natural action from which your instinct recoils. The worst moment in the aircraft is the opening of the door through which you jump. I dislike the sudden, furious howling of the slipstream as it storms outside the aperture, eliminat-ing all possibility of speech other than frantic shouting, and ready to toss you about like a leaf when you commit your body to it. But there is a bustle and feeling of purpose in an aircraft which are infinitely better than the clinical silence of the balloon.

On the whole I was surprised at how little I minded the whole performance, and now indeed rather enjoy a parachute jump. Although your nerve is supposed to deteriorate with age, and does in some respects do so, I am certain that if I had been twenty years younger I would have been much more frightened. In middle age you develop a more philosophical and resigned attitude which calms fluttering imagination; you possess a fatalism based on knowledge of the enormous odds against disaster. You are more instinctive and imaginative when young.

Parachuting and showjumping, with Rome only a few weeks distant, had to be combined, and normally could be with comparative ease provided I only rode on Saturdays. On one Saturday, however, it was necessary, owing to bad weather earlier in the week, to fit in two jumps. I accordingly found myself jumping from an aircraft at seven in the morning, and again at ten, and on Workboy at Taplow Show at one. I do not recommend the combination of these two activities in one day; parachuting is not good for your showjumping eye.

If I saw more of it I believe Rome would oust Paris as my favourite foreign city. It is of absorbing interest and immense charm; the shops, not impossibly expensive, are of infinite variety and taste. The International Horse Show takes place in the Piazza di Siena, loveliest of arenas, in the Borghese Gardens. Even the rain did not spoil it, and nor did it surprise the Italians, for it always rains for the Horse Show. The Italian Minister for Agriculture some days earlier, in outlining plans to cope with a threatened drought, had besought his audience to be of good cheer ". . . for next week is the Horse Show, and so there will be no drought."

The Rome courses were tricky rather than formidable; some of the distances in the combinations were much more awkward than any we were used to meeting at home. We were short of Pat Smythe and David Broome and, to begin with, short of success. This was unusually worrying because the Show coincided with our Queen's state visit to Rome, and on *Grand Prix* day she was due to pay the Show a visit. George Hobbs could not ride Royal Lord, who was lame, and of the others only Workboy was jumping up to form.

One by one the great Italians and their horses faulted in the *Gran Premio di Roma,* the big individual competition of the week. Raimondo d'Inzeo with the Olympic champion Posilippo, as well as Gowran Girl and Merano; Piero d'Inzeo with The Rock and Sunbeam, all fell by the way-side in the first round. Mancinelli with Rockette remained as the sole Italian clear round. Ringrose of Ireland had clears with Cloyne and Loch an Espaig; so did a French-man and a German. The British horses all made errors, mostly small, except Workboy, as usual at his best on the big occasion, who jumped a confident clear. I left the ring with a deep feeling of relief. At least the Queen, when she arrived for the final, would see one Union Jack being carried round.

She arrived, the crowd rose to our national anthem, and the jump-off began before a packed and excited crowd. The rain held off. Ringrose dashed round on Cloyne in very fast time—clear. Workboy was next in, with only one aim, to gallop. We went round as hard as we could go and I do not believe it would have been possible for my gallant sixteen-year-old to have jumped that big course any faster. Though we were clear, to my great disappointment Cloyne was fractionally quicker. Mancinelli and Rockette made a desperate bid for Italy but dropped a foot in the water. Ringrose then put the first prize firmly in the bag by beat-ing Cloyne's time on Loch an Espaig, leaving us third. As the Queen walked round with the rosettes she seemed, from her smile, pleased to recognise some comparatively familiar British figures in the line-up.

Workboy put up another good performance in the Nations' Cup, for which there was an imposing course. He was the best British horse on the day, with Mary Barnes on Sudden in brave and close support. Workboy had the same honour later in the season at Dublin, when in the Aga Khan Cup he shared the honours in the British team with Scorchin.

Our first engagement after our return was Windsor Show, and here Workboy jumped in his best form until the floodlights were turned on for the final. They were not the best of floodlights but most horses found them bright enough. Soon after we began our round it became quite obvious that Workboy could not focus the fences. After flattening the first four I realised something was wrong, and withdrew. I tried again the next night, with the same results. Cursing, almost certainly unfairly, the Windsor floodlights, I took him home.

He was still jumping very well in daylight, and was selected for the British team at the White City. Here I resolved he must try again in artificial light, for most of the big competitions were at night and I knew the floodlights at the White City were first class. We qualified for the King George V Cup and I awaited the test with some anxiety. He started his round tensely and was jumping very big and nervously. At every fence he seemed to become more worried, and instead of settling to our round I found myself growing steadily more unhappy as we progressed, clear though we were jumping. Suddenly at some barrels in the middle of the ring he stopped. I turned him round and he reluctantly jumped them. The next fence was a big combination, and he refused to go near it. Ignominiously we left the ring, eliminated for three refusals, in an atmosphere of silent sympathy from the crowd which had cheered us so vigorously a year before.

It seemed certain from this, and from other signs I had noticed, that Workboy's eyesight had deteriorated. I tested his heart in case that should be causing the trouble, but it still wheezed on at the same tempo which had survived probably all of six seasons' jumping and an unknown number of steeplechases. I continued jumping him, but never again under floodlights, and he won many more prizes. At Dublin, back for the first time in the land of his birth, he gained countless admirers and friends, and was in top form. But as we rode out of the Ballsbridge ring at the end of the show, I had decided that the rosette beside those two eager black ears, cocked as if on the gallops twelve years before, should be the last for which we would compete abroad.

I had no regrets at this decision. Workboy would next year be seventeen. He could still jump in the top class; but the winnings of the present season, well down on those of the two previous, were the writing on the wall. His international days were coming to an end; let them, I felt, finish now instead of flickering out by degrees. It was, too, time I finished. Many Army officers only heard of me when I was engaged in some non-military activity, and saw me only on the television screen on Workboy's back. Some of them wondered whether I ever did any soldiering. When a General met me one day and said breezily, "Well, how's Sandhurst?—Oh, I forgot, you're never there," the words, jokingly meant, struck home. It was not enough, it seemed, for me to know my duty was done; it must be seen to be done. The red light shone, dimly but unmistakably. Henceforth Workboy and I would jump at local shows, when and where we liked.

It was pleasant in the spring of 1962 to know that there was no hurry, no deadline by which Workboy must be ready. He was well and cheerful, though signs of age were beginning to show. He jumped with his usual abandon in our practice sessions, until just as the season was about to begin he ricked his back through showing off—over a very small fence which he pretended was an obstacle in a *Grand Prix* and cleared by a yard. He then became very sorry for himself, and was out of action for a month. I reflected that this was the first time in seven seasons that he had been unable to jump when I wanted him to.

We missed the popular Ascot Show, but I aimed to make a start at Aldershot a fortnight later. Two days before it I gave him a final test of his back, and found him fully recovered. I had been riding a novice horse while Workboy was laid up, and it was a real pleasure to feel my old friend beneath me again, to revel in his elegant flashing stride and to feel in his turns and response the result of years of training and experience together. No longer did he make wild leaps into space, all now was timed, regulated and controlled; quick brain and wiry body in harmony. We soared round a practice course, turned sharp and flicked perfectly over a five-foot rail. That was enough, he was fit again. Tomorrow a quiet exercise with his groom, and the next day back into the front line. I walked him home quietly, happy to resume our partnership.

Next morning I passed Workboy's box just as he had been made ready for exercise with his groom. His coat gleamed black, and with arched neck and ferocious mien he made his usual pretence of savaging me. I laughed at him, commented on how well he looked, and went indoors to my breakfast. Ten minutes later there were thunderous knocks on the front door. On opening it I beheld, panting and dishevelled, one of the stablemen. He pointed to a distant wood. "Workboy's collapsed—over there!" he cried. We got the Landrover and drove off. With the Olympic vet's prediction breaking surface in my mind, I knew what we would see. As we approached, his groom's distraught face told me all I needed to know. The black coat was dull and lifeless, his body seemed to have shrunk. Just an old, dead horse stretched out upon the ground.

Epilogue

THE passing of Workboy was not only a personal loss, it meant that the tempo of my showjumping life, instead of being merely reduced, ceased altogether. The change was abrupt, but probably in many ways for the best.

Showjumping, and not only international showjumping by a long chalk, has become very nearly a full-time occupation. To practise it with success you must either have a farm or business which can for long periods be entrusted to someone else, or have no need to earn your living, or earn it indirectly from showjumping by some method which sustains your amateur status (the amateur/professional distinction in showjumping, with its big cash prizes, is probably more absurd than in any other sport—and more impossible to define). I can see little likelihood of a personal comeback, but you never know.

Becalmed, I soldier on with no other horizon in sight. I may see one soon, I may not. Meanwhile in a thoroughly middle-aged way I remind myself of the past. I am strictly forbidden by my wife to display too many riding photographs—"It makes the house look so horsy"—and I agree with her. Ronnie Cronin jumping the Chair at Aintree is allowed, so are Pointsman and Mandarin coming over the last fence at Kempton, but Rareweed has been banished to the smallest room.

The hard-won Pentathlon medals still nestle in their cases; they are carted about from place to place and although we have always meant to put them up somewhere we have never actually done so. Now and again I turn out a boxroom and trip over an old canvas, ill-painted but evocative reminder of early struggles. The Gold Cup which Pointsman won on the great day at Sandown seems to have turned silver with age . . . My Chilean trophy gleams bronze. Workboy, beautifully painted by Joan Wanklyn, looks down from the wall.

School athletic cups, pictures of ponies, children's show and gymkhana rosettes, are joining the mementoes of middle age as my sons grow up. Two generations together. The best years are yet to come.